SHARECROPPER'S
WISDOM

Dee,
There is no power greater than the
human spirit when it catches on fire.
Flame On !!! JRG 9/17/16

GENERAL J.R. GORHAM

LAEL PUBLISHING

SHARECROPPER'S WISDOM
by General J.R. Gorham
Co-written by Patty Jo Sawvel
Published by Lael Publishing, LLC
Winston Salem, North Carolina
www.LaelPublishing.com

ISBN 978-0-9916515-2-8

Cover Designer and Design Director:
Angela Singletary Huntley

For more information visit the author's websites:
www.GeneralJRGorham.com or
www.SharecroppersWisdom.com or
www.TheGorhamGroup.net

First Edition

Printed in the United States of America.

DEDICATION

To my parents, Roy and Madie Gorham, who successfully raised seven children on meager sharecropper's wages, supplemented with huge helpings of practical wisdom. They loyally passed on to their children three keys to success—hard work, strict discipline, and Godly principles. Thanks Momma and Daddy. I love you.

ACKNOWLEDGEMENTS

To my lovely wife, Barbara, who provided me with amazing support and flexibility during the writing of this book. What an honor it has been to share my life with you. You have stayed with me through the good, the bad, and the ugly. I love you.

To my children, Tony, Jamie and Joshua—you are blessings from God. You have helped me to understand the relationships between love, happiness, giving and receiving. You inspire me to set a good example to help you negotiate this maze called life. I love you.

To my siblings, Joyce, Lillie, Sarah, Madie, Vickie, and Walter—what a glorious journey we have shared! Thank you for your individual contributions to this project. Daddy and Momma are in heaven smiling, knowing that we worked together to make this book a reality. I love you.

To my cousin, Charieese Sutton, and niece, Cassandra Bell—thanks for proofing sections of this book and for your love, encouragement, advice, and support. I love you both.

To the community of Falkland, North Carolina—especially my church family at St. John Missionary Baptist Church. You provided rich and nourishing soil for my soul. Thank you for your love, support, and encouragement, which helped shape me into the person I have become. There is no place like home.

To my spiritual parents, Bishop James and Joyce Hash—who partnered with God to teach me about love, the listening side of prayer, and the need to have hope (joyful, confident,

expectations). You have left your residue in my spirit. I love you both.

And finally, to my Lord and Savior Jesus Christ. He is responsible for all that I am and all that I hope to be. He is not done with me yet! The best is yet to come. I love you, Lord.

ENDORSEMENTS

"An absorbing account of one man's journey toward a future filled with rich reward, told with courage and vivid descriptions of a life transformed at the hand of his sharecropper father."

Cassandra Bell
Author of Mississippi Blues, After the Storm,
News Anchor WITN-TV

"Sharecropper's Wisdom is good storytelling packed with rich, memorable life lessons, humorous anecdotes and practical wisdom."

Virginia D. Hardy, PhD
Vice Chancellor for Student Affairs
East Carolina University

"Sharecropper's Wisdom is a must read for aspiring leaders— especially young people. His father's frank and down to earth advice gave J.R. Gorham the wisdom to navigate the most challenging military and civilian opportunities. It was my pleasure to serve as his Colonel and to witness his transformation into a role model General and lifelong friend known for his leadership, character, and integrity."

Gary Pendleton
Brigadier General (Ret.)

"Sharecropper's Wisdom is a powerful proof that success and happiness are not dependent on material wealth, but rather, on fulfilling our moral duty to God, family, and neighbors. This father— a role model for all— demonstrates the power of using faith, love and wisdom to motivate and inspire the next generation to new levels of greatness."

Bryan E. Beatty
Former Secretary of the NC Department of Public Safety

CONTENTS

FOREWORD

How does a small town African American boy nicknamed "Hippie" grow up to become a General in the U.S. Armed Services? What was the primary source of inspiration for him to achieve such a distinguished leadership role in America, especially given his upbringing in the rural South in the 1960s and 1970s when the lines of racial inequality were clearly demarcated in the sandy loam soils of the region? In this highly engaging treatise, General James R. Gorham (JR) provides important, timely, and useful answers to both of these questions.

JR focuses in laser-like fashion on the key driver of his success as a high ranking military officer, commercial banker, civil servant in state government, and most important to him,

husband and father. Contrary to what you might expect, he does not attribute his successes in life to leadership lessons he learned from any one of the entities that appears on TrainingIndustry. com's annual listing of the top twenty Leadership Training Companies. Rather, in intimate and oftentimes riveting prose, JR carefully chronicles the lessons he learned from a wise man from the East, that is, east of Interstate 95—arguably the poorest region of the state—and specifically from the Town of Falkland, a small farming community roughly eight miles west of the county seat of Greenville in Pitt County, North Carolina.

The wise man was JR's father, who was a sharecropper by occupation but a tenacious, visionary, and God-fearing leader in every other walk of life. For JR's father, no matter how difficult times were, the glass was always half full even when it was half empty. Because of this optimistic or hopeful outlook, he was affectionately known as Mr. Roy "Joy" Gorham in the Falkland community.

Mr. Roy "Joy" was a gentleman's gentleman. He went to great lengths to not only take care of his immediate and extended family but also seemingly everyone else in the community as well—from the town drunk in need of a safe ride home at midnight to the little old lady in need of firewood to heat her home in the winter. But it would have been a mistake to take his kindness as a weakness. Mr. Roy "Joy" was also a man's man. When it came to matters of racial injustice and inequality, Mr. Roy Joy did not scratch where he did not itch. He was one of

Falkland's premier drum-majors for justice and equality in all walks of life, especially public education.

This book is chocked full of leadership lessons that a son, JR, gleaned from his sharecropper father, Mr. Roy "Joy", while growing up during the turbulent 1960s and 1970s. Unfortunately, there are far too many young people of color today who are growing up in communities—urban and rural—that are not unlike the Falkland community of a half century ago—poverty stricken, geographically isolated, and economically marginalized from mainstream America. And sadly, far too many of these young people who find themselves in this circumstance do not have the benefit of access to sage advice and direction from a contemporary equivalent of Mr. Roy "Joy". Because the leadership lessons conveyed in this book are just as relevant today as they were a half century ago, it should be mandatory reading for anyone who is a key influencer in the lives of young people of color today.

As a fellow native son of Falkland, NC, I want to thank and commend JR for writing this very insightful and thought-provoking book. Reading the manuscript made me realize that I am a collateral beneficiary of his father's wisdom. Somehow the leadership lessons that JR attributes to his father became deeply engrained in the DNA of the entire Falkland community. Thus, I can honestly and thankfully say that, like JR, I am a much better man today as a consequence of exposure to the rules of life as espoused by Mr. Roy "Joy" Gorham, a sage old sharecropper

from east of Interstate 95 in North Carolina—God's country.

James H. Johnson, Jr., Ph.D.
Kenan Distinguished Professor of Strategy & Entrepreneurship
Kenan-Flagler Business School
University of North Carolina at Chapel Hill

INTRODUCTION

Originally, I began writing this book to preserve Daddy's powerful wisdom. His wisdom, gleaned from life as a sharecropper, propelled me to the top of military and business careers. My intention was to give this inheritance—worth more than gold—to my children, their children, and all the future grands that I would not have a chance to meet.

However, as I listened to young people and even seasoned leaders around the world, it became clear that character-building wisdom is needed and wanted by a vast array of people.

So, I broadened the historical context—while retaining my boyhood antics—to demonstrate the ripple effect of one person's leadership and the powerful impact it can have on family, community, and country.

SHARECROPPER'S WISDOM

Through the pages of this book, readers will join Daddy in the fields growing the 13-month crop—tobacco—and all the hard work that goes along with it. Together, we'll sort out the social structure of the little Southern town called Falkland. Then, from this vantage point, we'll witness the painful birth of that beautiful baby called civil rights.

Each chapter contains seeds of wisdom neatly wrapped in a story:

- Your word is one thing that you give and you keep at the same time.
- Be a giver, not a taker.
- You're becoming your company.
- It isn't ever as bad as it first appears.

My goal is to help people see themselves as a part of the bigger picture and to understand that true leadership begins by leading oneself. My method is to share the wisdom of master teacher, Roy Gorham, and his toughest pupil—me.

Chapter 1

THE LIFE OF A SHARECROPPER

y daddy was a sharecropper. In 1956, the year that he and Momma welcomed me into the world, while the rest of the country was enjoying an economic boom complete with rock 'n roll, the impending space race with the development of Sputnik 1, and classic films like *The Man Who Knew Too Much*, our family was living in a four-room house with no running water.

Somehow, as the rest of the world rushed forward, our family stayed firmly locked in the year 1865. That was when slavery ended and sharecropping began. Sharecropping—it

*The young sharecropper,
Roy Gorham*

Young Madie Gray Gorham

*Me, James Roy Gorham in
3rd grade.*

*My brother, Walter Louis
Gorham in
1st grade.*

is said—is one step beyond slavery. Because I lived it, I can explain it.

As slaves—the master owns everything; you, the land, the houses, the crops, the profits, your children—everything! When the Civil War ended slavery in 1865, many "masters" didn't have the money or the inclination to pay their former slaves, so they offered them the opportunity to sharecrop. By definition, sharecrop means to share the crop and its profits.

In our family, Mr. Kinchen Robert "K. R." Wooten of Falkland (Pitt County), North Carolina owned the 40 acres we farmed (one acre is approximately the size of a football field between the goal lines), the house we lived in, the mules we used to plow, the coupons to the store he owned, the seed, and the fertilizer. Daddy and his children did all the farm work as Daddy's "share" of the deal. So, from February to November we plowed, planted, weeded, cultivated, harvested and cured about 6 acres of tobacco, with the remaining 34 acres producing corn and peanuts.

Following the sale of the final crop in November— tobacco being our most profitable by far—Mr. Wooten claimed one-half of the profits right off the top. This was called the 50/50 plan. Then, from Daddy's half, Mr. Wooten deducted the following; one year's rent for our 4-room uninsulated shack, rent for the mules, the cost of the seed and fertilizer, reimbursement for money we borrowed to pay workers to help bring in the harvest, reimbursement for the coupons that we used to buy

provisions at the W.W. Wooten store, and any other expenses we had incurred. The tiny remaining profit belonged to my daddy.

Now I can't say for sure, but it seems that when Daddy had a big harvest, Mr. Wooten's charges against his account went up accordingly. Daddy had no access to the books, so he never really knew how much Mr. Wooten was charging him. But whatever the case, it seemed like Daddy never got ahead.

Now you would think that an arrangement like that would make an honest and hardworking man angry, but Daddy never complained. This was the work that his family had done for generations—either as slaves or as free men and he was proud that he knew how to do it and do it well.

Daddy also knew that money was not the only currency of exchange and that stockpiled material assets were not a reliable measure of a man.

Though he had very little cash, Daddy always managed to buy an old broken down car. Often times, he would trade his labor or some pigs and chicks—which did not come under the sharecropper agreement—for items he wanted.

Daddy then used the car to serve his community. He drove people to the doctors, transported one talented young girl back and forth to East Carolina University for advanced music lessons, helped widows get their groceries, and drove the choir at St. John's Missionary Baptist Church to surrounding churches to perform. Daddy did this all free of charge—earning him the honorable designation of "Taxicab."

Then, when his brother Sim suffered his third stroke, leaving him unable to work or speak, Daddy invited him and Aunt Blanche into our home. So, we had 11 people living in a four-room house with no running water. Daddy and Momma shared one bedroom and my baby brother, Walt, slept on their sofa. Uncle Sim and Aunt Blanche shared the next bedroom, and Vickie Lynn slept on their sofa. My four sisters and I (James Roy Gorham) shared the other bedroom. In the bed, Lillie Gray and Sarah Elizabeth slept with the heads at the top of the bed and I slept between them with my head at the foot of the bed. Joyce C. and Madie Sue shared the sofa in the room. We slept this way until I reached the age of 10. Then, I had to sleep in the kitchen, our fourth room.

You see, despite Daddy's cramped circumstances, he was a generous man. Daddy was as refreshing as a spring rain. In fact, my dad, Roy Gorham, was fondly nicknamed Roy Joy. And what grew out of his heart was a very rare strain of wisdom that nurtured the leaders of tomorrow—Sharecropper's Wisdom. It's time to share Daddy's wisdom with you.

The house of Bud Peaden. It has the same floor plan as the home where I was born. Both houses were built at the same time.

24

Chapter 2

YOU CAN'T HAVE ONE

Even though my daddy married at the age of 24, he continued to live like a single man—smoking, drinking, and running around—until he was 35 years old. By that time, he and Momma had experienced the joy of bringing five healthy girls into the world and endured the tragic loss of their firstborn son, Roy Gorham, Jr. Their newborn suffered multiple birth defects and only lived a few days.

Perhaps through the hope or the comfort imparted by the scriptures, Daddy gave his life to Christ and joined the St. John's Missionary Baptist Church. He abruptly quit smoking, drinking, seeing other women, and playing cards. The next year,

I was born into the new soil of his heart. He was determined to "rule his house properly" so that he could qualify to "serve in the house of the Lord" as a deacon.

I dig up this dirt for many reasons. My daddy's life provides powerful proof that a man can change. It also demonstrates that different children in the same family can experience very different upbringings. Lastly, the Daddy I knew never smoked—and I never bought a pack of cigarettes in my life. But, Daddy did farm tobacco until the last day of his life. The tobacco plant is so deeply rooted into our family history, that it would be impossible to share Daddy's wisdom without sharing his life's work.

The tobacco seed is tiny, smaller than a grain of salt. In fact, 10,000 seeds fit into a teaspoon. Beginning in February, Daddy sprinkled seeds on a special plot of land called our seedbed. It was about as long as a football field and 10 feet wide. Then, he carefully covered the plot with plastic to keep it as warm as possible and waited for the seeds to germinate. Once that happened, tiny green leaves appeared. Shortly after that, Daddy switched out the plastic for cloth so that the plants could flourish.

Now farmers with smaller seedbeds traditionally have to thin the plants—painstakingly removing weaklings so that the most robust plants can have access to all the nutrients in the soil. This is particularly difficult because seedling tobacco plants are fragile and their roots tend to tangle. However, for many

farmers, thinning the beds is the best way to ensure a profitable crop. Instead of doing this, Daddy overplanted—using a huge seedbed—and then used about 25% of the plants that germinated to transplant into our fields.

Though Daddy didn't use the "thinning" process with tobacco, he did use it as a parenting tool. He plucked out undesirable inclinations from the soil of my heart so that my better inclinations could flourish. To better understand my "inclinations," I'll need to share the home atmosphere that I was born into.

I was born into the love and affection of five little girls who'd never had a healthy baby brother. There was Joyce C. age nine, Lillie Gray age eight, Sarah Elizabeth age six, Madie Sue age four, and finally Vickie Lynn age three. They kissed my little feet, fanned flies from my smiling face, fed me, sang to me, encouraged me, and altogether made me the center of their world. To this day, I credit them with giving me the self-esteem and confidence to do everything in life I set my heart on.

Understandably then, I wanted to be just like them. So when I was about three years old, I watched excitedly as Momma combed a beautiful ponytail into the hair of each of my sisters. They looked so pretty that I wanted one too.

I waited patiently, all smiles and said, "I want one too, Momma."

All the girls giggled and Momma laughed too. But I didn't laugh. I was serious. I wanted a ponytail.

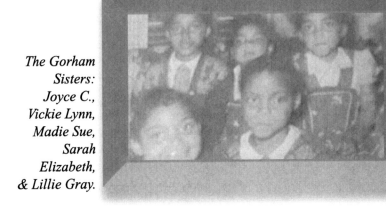

The Gorham Sisters: Joyce C., Vickie Lynn, Madie Sue, Sarah Elizabeth, & Lillie Gray.

I pleaded, "I want a ponytail!"

Now had my daddy not heard all the ruckus and stepped into the room, they may have indulged me just for the fun of it. But, that never happened.

Daddy didn't smile. He bluntly said, "You can't have one."

I begged and cried and stubbornly carried on.

Daddy finally added, "You're a boy. Boys don't wear ponytails."

That was the end of that. No one argued with Daddy.

The next year, our crops did well and we had a nice Christmas. At first light, my sisters and I raced into Momma and Daddy's bedroom. The girls with their gowns flowing and me in my LCDs (long cotton drawers). Neatly set against the wall was a present for each child, and at the foot of that present was a shoebox.

We all knew what was in the shoebox. Daddy had been to the W.W. Wooten Store and bought a box of apples, a box of oranges, a bag of tangerines, and a delicious assortment of candy, which might include chocolate covered peanuts, candy orange slices, peanut brittle, and something we called Christmas Raisins.

Some assortment of those goodies were in each shoebox. But, it was always a surprise to run into the room to see what our gift would be. Joyce C. went first. She didn't have to tear off any wrapping paper, because we never had any, but we all watched as she carefully took her brand new baby doll out of the store bought box. Joyce C. oohed and aahed and after gazing into her baby's eyes, she gave her baby the most loving hug. I watched intently as each of my sisters freed and embraced their very own baby. It was almost like watching a movie. Indeed, when they hugged their baby doll, it was almost as if they were hugging me, Bro (my nickname is pronounced "brah" as in brother).

Then it was my turn. I could see clearly what lay against the wall. It wasn't a soft and cuddly baby doll. No, it was a cold, dumb toy pistol. I couldn't hide my disappointment. I didn't even want to open it. I asked sadly, "Where's my baby doll?"

My sincere reaction took everyone by surprise, but my dad quickly set things straight. He said, "Bro, you can't have one. Boys don't play with dolls. You have a pistol."

Then my daddy helped me open the package and load

the roll of paper caps. It didn't take me long to recover from my heartbreak. I was a pretty active preschooler and I loved the noise—pop, pop, pop—and the sweet smell of sulfur. Within minutes, I became genuinely intrigued by my cap gun. And soon, my baby brother Walt—18 months younger than me—was old enough to wrestle and join me in my boyhood adventures.

But this "weeding out" process—realizing that I couldn't have certain things, understanding boundaries and differences—helped me as I got older. Just like Daddy said "no" to me, I learned to say "no" to myself. Over time, I learned to say no to lying, stealing, cheating—weeding out behaviors that could keep me from growing up to be the man that I wanted to be.

Also, when friends from school invited me to their house for a party, I could say "no" because I knew that if I went to their house, one day I'd have to invite them to my house.

I didn't want anyone to know that I lived in a little four-bedroom house with 11 people and no indoor plumbing. I also didn't want them to know that we didn't even have 11 forks or 11 glasses to drink from.

The truth is: I loved my family, but I was deeply ashamed of the way that we lived. We were among the poorest people in our community. We were one of the few families that depended 100% on sharecropping for our income.

Chapter 3

IT AIN'T EVER AS BAD AS IT FIRST APPEARS

My big day had finally arrived. For years, I'd watched as my sisters left for school, leaving me behind. I was always assured that when I turned six, it would be my turn to go.

I slipped into my newly washed hand-me down dungarees (today known as blue jeans), a red plaid flannel shirt, and my orange brogans (durable high-topped split leather boots originally worn by soldiers, slaves, and sharecroppers).

I felt excited and ready for school. I'd learned my

ABCs and 123s watching Captain Kangaroo on Aunt Blanche's television. Aunt Blanche had a day job and she had owned all the technology in our house. She and Uncle Sim had a hot plate, a television, and telephone in their room. We children called their bedroom the "entertainment room," and they generously shared their blessings with their nieces and nephews. In fact, they really helped to raise us because they took care of us when Momma and Daddy were out visiting the sick in the evenings.

Aside from the television, I had my five sisters to make sure that their little brother was going to school well prepared. One of my sisters, Sarah Elizabeth, read books all the time and dreamed of being a teacher one day, so I had plenty of schooling at home.

However, almost immediately after I arrived at Bruce Falkland Elementary School, the excitement vanished from my little body as quickly as a rare piece of candy in my pocket.

"Where are my sisters?" I asked my Daddy nervously.

"They're all going to their classes," my Daddy said as he walked me to the first grade classroom. We didn't have kindergarten back in 1962. Our first grade was first grade.

"Well, where are Mitchell and Dexter (Lane)?"

My daddy looked at me for a moment. He was a man of few words, but he could see that my courage was fading fast. As we stopped at the door to Mrs. Clark's room, Daddy said, "They go to the school for white children."

I put on my brakes. I didn't want to go in. I didn't know

anybody. This was the first time I'd ever been separated from my parents and suddenly this didn't seem like such a good idea.

Bruce Falkland Elementary School where all my siblings and I attended.

My voice quivered and I pleaded, "I want to go home."

In a rare display of gentleness, my daddy grasped me by the shoulders, bent down and while looking me straight in the eyes said, "Boy, it ain't ever as bad as it first appears."

Then, he firmly guided me inside the door and promised, "You'll be alright once you get in there."

And there I was. Facing the unknown. My eyes darted around the room frantically, looking for one familiar face. Just when I was ready to turn back for the door, I found him. Rick Streeter!

Just a few days prior, there had been a death at the Dupree's, our neighbors. Buddy Hemby, the black funeral director had prepared the body and then, according to custom,

he set the casket up in the families front room.

Our family, like many families, attended the wake—a time for prayer, comfort, and visitation before the funeral. The adults all went into the front room with the casket, but I didn't want any part of that. I'd heard the older folks talk about haints (a Southern term meaning haunted) and ghosts. I was afraid of dead people.

So while the grown folks comforted each other inside, I poked around outside. Then, I saw a little guy my age. He laughed easily and soon we were talking as if we'd known each other our whole lives. And now, here he was again!

He spotted me about the same time that I saw him— he being equally relieved to find one person that he knew. We quickly "manned up" and were ready for this adventure called school.

After that, I looked forward to going to school. I knew that the yellow bus was taking me to see my best friend and that was good enough. In time, I made more friends, though Rick Streeter and I remained best friends for life. In fact, to this day, Rick and I talk twice a week, on Mondays and Fridays.

Daddy was right. It ain't ever as bad as it first appears. I permanently engraved those words on the tablet of my heart. Over the years as I continued to be confronted with tests, trials, or tragedies, I called on that wisdom to give me the courage to step into the unknown. So far, it has always proved true.

Chapter 4

YOU BETTER PUT A HANDLE ON THAT

The tiny town of Falkland—occupying just one-quarter square mile—was incorporated in 1887. Built on the rich soil of the inner banks of coastal North Carolina, Falkland is deeply rooted in agriculture.

For many years, Falkland's two greatest claims to fame occurred about 20 years prior to its formal designation as a town.

During the Civil War, Union General Edward E. Potter approached Otter Creek Bridge to cross with his cavalrymen. Anticipating this, Confederate Major Thomas Claiborne cleverly burned the bridge and positioned 150 Confederate soldiers—mostly sharpshooters—on the eastern side of the creek. However, this promising ambush quickly derailed when Major Claiborne

fired shots prematurely, warning Union soldiers of the trap. Nonetheless, a one-hour engagement ensued. Thus, on July 19, 1863 the Famous Otter Creek Bridge Skirmish found its place in the pages of Falkland history.

Four years later, Captain Bryant Smith of Falkland secured a patent for the cotton planter and is credited with revolutionizing the cotton industry. Incidentally, the next year, 1868, North Carolina was readmitted to the Union.

However, since its founding and up to today, Falkland has never had many residents. In fact, Falkland reached its peak population in 1940—boasting 188 men, women, and children— the year before the United States entered World War II.

The year I was born—according the closest census in 1960—there were 140 residents. It was amazing that each and every citizen knew his place, including me. My daddy—like most daddies of the time—carefully taught his children the language, the look, and to some degree, the legacy of respect.

I remember when I was about six years old. We were sitting around the dinner table. Daddy didn't talk much, but sometimes he'd share an observation.

Daddy said, "Bud Peaden is planting his tobacco tomorrow."

Bud Peaden was a neighboring white sharecropper. He and Daddy helped each other out. Wanting a little attention, I piped up, "Daddy, why is Bud Peaden…"

Before I could finish, Daddy turned on me and said

sternly, "Boy, you better put a handle on that."

I knew exactly what he meant. I apologized and said, "I mean, why is Mr. Bud Peaden…"

In time, I figured out the language. As a black child, I had to address white people with either a Mr. or Miss before their name. I also answered their questions with a respectful "yes sir" or "no ma'am." Actually, I was expected to answer every adult—black or white—with this formal reply.

However, when it came to the black community, I mostly used the handle "cousin" which we actually pronounced as cuttin'. Even though we weren't really related—children showed respect for black adults by calling them cousin. So our neighbor up the road—Charlie Dupree—was actually called Cousin Dupree, which we then morphed to Cuttin' Dupree, and ultimately shortened to Cuttin' Pree. His wife, Beatrice, was fondly called Cuttin' Bea.

However, there were exceptions to these rules. For instance, Clarence Bembry was a black adult, but I didn't call him Cuttin' Bembry, Cuttin' Bem, or Cuttin' Bry. That's because he'd been to college and he was a teacher.

This was especially amazing because he was born in 1910, nine years before my daddy, at a time when it was highly unusual for a black man to attain higher education. So he was Mr. Bembry to me because even though he was black, he'd earned a higher handle. His wife automatically received a matching handle. To me, she was Miss Gleaner (Bembry). So the rule of

thumb was—when black people make something of themselves by means of education or a profession, they deserved a higher handle.

On the flip side, a few adults didn't deserve any handle at all. It was okay with Daddy if I called them by their first names. These people were the town drunks or people of bad reputation. So even as a child, I was allowed to call the two town drunks "Big Man Jones," or John Larry Dupree because they forfeited any status in the community.

All of these handles made life simple. At all times, I— James Roy Gorham— knew who I was in comparison to any other person. I also knew that it was up to me to earn a handle because in Falkland, NC, every black child begins life without a handle. The only person a child addressed by first name was another child. Because everyone in town—black and white, rich and poor—accepted and enforced the concept of handles, people mostly got along fine.

This idea of rank and respect was also taught at our dinner table every night. On the rare occasion that we had chicken for dinner, Momma and Daddy ate the breasts, my sisters divided the legs, thighs, and wings, and I got the last thing that jumped over the fence. My prize was the tail and the two little medallions of meat on the back.

As my sisters grew up, graduated, and moved out—I carried more of the workload and eventually earned the meat higher up on the chicken. In the meantime, I learned to fill up

on beans and biscuits.

One day, my daddy showed me a different kind of handle. There were no words. It was a way.

The main streets of Falkland are laid out like an "X." We lived on Highway 222 on the upper left arm of the X. The Wootens strategically owned both plots of land where Main Street crosses Highway 222. At the northern vortex, Mr. W. W. Wooten owned the W.W. Wooten Store. The southern vortex was dominated by the big, beautiful two-story home belonging to his Uncle K. R. Wooten. It was one of the finest homes in Falkland.

My father slowed his smoking pick-up truck to a halt around the back of Mr. Wooten's house and said, "Boy, you stay in the truck."

Of course, that caught my attention. I wanted to see what I was missing. So I watched carefully and quietly through the splintered windshield. Then, I saw my daddy do the strangest thing.

He walked up to the back door of the Wooten house, knocked, and then stepped back out into the yard. He waited a good long while, looking down and biding his time patiently.

After a spell, Mr. W. W. Wooten came out and the two men talked in the backyard.

I'm not sure what they talked about. Likely, it had to do with the crops, because Mr. W. W. Wooten, the nephew of Mr. K. R. Wooten, was caring for the sharecropping interests

as his uncle aged. What I noticed most was the way my daddy addressed him and how differently my daddy held himself. Clearly, Daddy talked to him differently than Daddy talked to Mr. Bud Peaden who was also a white man. And, by the way, Mr. Bud Peaden came in our front door and we went in his. We also ate food from each other's tables. We were black and he was white, but apparently, we were of the same rank because we were both sharecroppers.

When my daddy finished, he got back in the truck and we drove home. Not a word passed between us. Only later, did I piece together that in 1963; a black man never approached the front door or stepped inside the house of a white person of any stature. In fact, though my daddy lived until July 7, 1983, he never did step foot in the Wooten house.

However, a lot changed in those 20 years. I did go in that house, through the front door, and talked to Mr. W. W. Wooten face to face. But, that is another story for another time.

One thing is for sure: It was my daddy's diligent discipline regarding rank and respect that got me through the Wooten door and every other door of opportunity in my life. I clearly understood how to treat others and how to earn the respect that I desired.

Before my 55th birthday, I'd secured the handle of Brigadier General in the North Carolina National Guard—the first black man to achieve this rank in NC; Vice-President of First Citizens Bank in Kernersville, North Carolina (starting this

journey as the first black bank manager in the town's history), and most coveted, I have three children who lovingly bestow upon me the same handle that I gave to this sharecropper—Daddy.

The home of Woodrow W. Wooten, Falkland NC

SHARECROPPER'S WISDOM

Chapter 5

BOY, DON'T LIE TO ME

My daddy was a man of his word. If he said he was going to do something, then the whole community—black and white—knew that Roy Gorham was going to do it.

One family in our community—Cuttin' Pleasant and Cuttin' Bernice Jones—had a boy with disabilities. Little Charles was always sick and frequently crept close to death's door. The only thing my daddy could do to help was to bring an older woman—Louise "Dollbaby" Gorham—to sit with the child and comfort the family.

Daddy gave his word to the ailing family that whenever they needed Dollbaby's help—day or night—he would drive

her to their house. Now as often occurs, illnesses become more critical in the middle of the night.

So Daddy would work 12 hours in the blazing sun, exhausting every ounce of energy, slide into bed next to Momma, and the phone would ring. It might be 10 o'clock at night or it might be 2 o'clock in the morning. It didn't matter. Daddy pulled himself out of bed and kept his word.

And, he did it joyfully! He knew that Dollbaby, as a mother of the Church, could bring comfort to this hurting family. Dollbaby had endured the loss of her husband (my daddy's first cousin) at an early age and was raising 13 children. She understood the power of faith, hope, and love.

I think my daddy almost viewed keeping his word as a game or a personal challenge. He had an unbreakable rule. He told me, "Boy, your word is one thing that you give and you keep at the same time. Ain't too many things like that."

So no matter what happened, Daddy made himself keep his word. No excuses! He figured that if he gave his word, no matter how tired, how broke, or how anything he was—God would give him the means to keep his word. Daddy proved to himself over and over again that you can always keep your word.

It was honesty—and not a big house, fancy car, or huge bank account—that earned my daddy a stellar reputation in the community.

So you can imagine his dismay, when a store clerk told Daddy that his seven-year-old son had slipped some candy into his pocket without paying for it.

I remember the day clearly. Momma sent me to the Ernest Wooten Store—a one-man gas station/convenience store—to get a loaf of bread. While I was looking around, I spotted some candy. I wanted it, but I didn't have any money. I decided to slip a few pieces into my pocket.

I waited for Mr. Wooten to turn around, made my move, and then casually walked out of the store. Wow! Nothing happened. I thought I was pretty slick. I thought I got away with it.

*The Ernest Wooten store where I stole
candy at the age of seven.*

However, the next time my daddy went in the store, Mr. Ernest Wooten told him what I'd done.

When Daddy tracked me down, he lashed out at me like he was a tornado. It was not the typical pop on my butt for teasing my little brother Walt or for having to be called twice.

Daddy whipped me with his bare hands and his hands were huge. He had a working man's hands and wore a size 13 ring. I was a little runt, but little runt or not, he was not going to have a dishonest boy for a son.

Daddy said, "You don't pay for it, you don't take it."

He continued to beat me. I suppose by today's standards it would be child abuse, but in our community, it was the way things were. When the beating was done, I dragged my nearly lifeless body outside. I got away from the house and slumped in the sand.

Before long, the sun dried my tears and my power of reason began to revive. I decided that stolen candy wasn't free after all and I didn't like the price that I had to pay.

Now you would think that I would never steal again, but I do believe that I was the most stubborn pup my daddy had to raise.

It wasn't a few months later, when Daddy left his cup of coffee on the kitchen table. For a few moments, it had been just Daddy and I in the kitchen. I don't know where Momma was and I'm not sure where the other six kids were.

I watched Daddy sipping his coffee and knew the family rule. That was his coffee and there was no coffee for me. Momma and Daddy used to say, "Coffee will stunt your growth."

Now if I really believed that, I wouldn't have touched Daddy's coffee because I was a little runt. In school, I was always one of the smallest boys in my class. And at home, even when I was seven years old, my five-and-a-half year old brother, Walt, was already catching up with me.

Whatever the case, whenever I asked for a sip of coffee, I was told no. But you know how kids are. Sometimes when we are told, "Don't do it," our mischievous little minds say, "Go do it."

Soon enough, my opportunity arrived. Someone in the yard called for Daddy to come outside. Daddy took one more sip, sat his cup on the wooden table, and went outside.

There I was, alone with Daddy's cup of coffee. I thought, "This is my chance to see what this grown up drink is all about."

I looked at the cup and I looked at Daddy through the window. By now, he was well into the middle of the yard. I kept my eyes on him and quickly sipped out of his cup.

Frankly, I didn't think coffee was that great. Pepsi Cola or Kool aide—rare items in my house—were more my style. But, it didn't matter.

Daddy came back in the house, took one look at me and asked, "Boy, did you drink any of my coffee?"

Of course, I lied. "No Sir. I didn't touch it."

Daddy shot back quick as whip, "Boy, don't you lie to me! Did you touch my coffee?"

"No Sir! No Sir!"

He looked me in the eyes and said, "I KNOW you took some. I KNOW you took some of my coffee. YOU took a swallow of my coffee."

Before I knew it, his hands were punctuating his words across my face, my back, and my body. It was another beat down. This time, I'd broken two rules. I stole from my daddy and then lied about it.

As he was beating me, Daddy told me, "Boy, I'm always going to find out. Don't think you can do wrong and get away with it. I'm ALWAYS going to find out."

He was right. In anything that mattered, if I did wrong, he found out. And Daddy didn't let things slide. He had absolutely zero tolerance for lying, stealing, or cheating. The cure for that behavior was a beating, and no amount of pleading would keep him from training up his children the way he thought God wanted them to go.

It's interesting, because to this day I can't figure out how Daddy knew that I'd taken a sip of his coffee. Over the decades, I've replayed the scene in my mind hundreds of times. I know for sure that it was not due to how much I drank. I only had a tiny sip.

I wonder if maybe I spilled a little drop on the table. After

all, I was only seven and not a particularly careful little boy. Or, maybe Daddy noticed that the cup was moved. It would not be beyond Daddy to note exactly where he placed his cup on the table.

Whatever the case, that one incident taught me several lessons all balled up together. Don't lie. Don't steal—even at home. Expect Daddy to find out EVERYTHING. Oh, and I don't like coffee. I'm not sure if that is due to the beating or if I just never would have cared for the taste. But, I rarely drink more than a few sips of coffee.

Daddy was the same kind of watchdog with my five sisters. In fact, he was even worse. It was not that they got beat a lot. In fact, most of them could count their beatings from Daddy on one hand or even a few fingers. But, Daddy guarded them like a soldier protecting Fort Knox.

One time, my oldest sister, Joyce, was getting a ride home from a ballgame. She was in 9th grade and part of the marching band. Daddy found a "play brother" for Joyce and three other girls so they could be safely transported home.

As my sister, Joyce, explains, "A play brother is a trusted older boy who protects you like he is your brother. My play brother, Ronald Barnes, was three years older than me, and Daddy made it clear that he was only supposed to have me and the other three girls in the car."

All went well for many weeks. The young man faithfully held to his trust and delivered the girls to their homes flawlessly.

However, after one game, the girls all wanted their boyfriends to come along for the ride. It was harmless fun and they were sure that no one would ever find out. Ha!

Joyce told me, "We had four couples in the station wagon all hugged up and there was a dirt path near our home. Daddy's car was parked in the dirt path and when we drove by, he saw eight people silhouetted. He pulled out behind us and followed us into our driveway."

Daddy didn't beat the play brother, but he did fire him.

Chapter 6

THAT'S WHERE YOUR PLACE IS

S ummertime was working time for a sharecropper's family. As soon as the school year ended, it was time to pick cucumbers. We picked every other day and it was back breaking work. At least with tobacco, I'd get to stand up and walk to the truck with each armful of leaves. But with cucumbers, there was no reason to get up. We stayed bent over the whole morning, tossing cucumbers into buckets.

"You guys been missing cucumbers," Daddy said. "We want ones, twos, and threes. Not fours and definitely not jumbos."

It was hard to find them all. Cucumbers tend to hide under the leaves and blend into vegetation. It always surprised

me that I could be in the patch every other day for weeks on end and still, I'd come across a jumbo that finally demanded my attention by turning yellow or even orange. I knew that to get to be a number five, that cucumber had to first be a one, then a two, three, and four.

"The money is in the ones, twos, and threes," Daddy reminded us.

This was important. It wasn't just money for Daddy and the family. This was one of the few crops that Daddy paid us to pick. He didn't pay us much. It was a small percentage of the value of the pickings. But, it served as an incentive and gave us a little change in our pockets.

So I watched with great interest when Daddy ran my cucumbers through the grader. Daddy poured the cucumbers on a drop down, and as the machine shook cucumbers dropped progressively through narrowing slits according to their diameter.

I wanted as many cucumbers as possible to drop all the way down through the number one slit—because ones paid the most. As I watched this, year after year it dawned on me that cucumbers are a very unusual crop. With our other crops—tobacco, corn, soybeans, and peanuts—the bigger the leaf or seed, the bigger our profit. But with cucumbers, it was exactly the opposite.

When Daddy was paid, I was paid. On this particular day, we headed straight for Oscar Lee's Bar and Grill in the heart of Falkland. When we walked in the restaurant, Daddy

got to talking to another man, so I started wandering around. I was jingling the change in my pocket, thinking what a fortunate eight-year-old boy I was, when I walked right past the bar.

I thought, "Today, I'll sit in one of the chairs."

As soon as my fanny touched that chair, my daddy grabbed me up by the nape of the neck and said, "Boy, don't you ever sit down in that chair again. You need to get back there to the bar. That's where your place is."

Then he turned to the owner and said, "I am so sorry. He is such a foolish boy. That will never happen again. I'm so sorry."

I did as my daddy said, but I was thinking, "What is the big deal?"

Daddy ordered an ice cream cone for me. I ate it and we walked out the door as if nothing had ever happened. But, I never forgot it. Actions speak louder than words and what I heard loud and clear was that the bar at the back was for black folks and the four tables with four chairs each at the front of the restaurant were for whites only.

The following year, our family was helping Mr. Bud

Oscar Lee snack bar where Daddy snatched me up when I sat at the white only tables.

Peaden with his tobacco harvest. My sisters were complaining about the ugly green tobacco worms. They didn't want to touch the worms and they didn't want any worms touching them.

Mr. Peaden's 14-year-old nephew, William, heard the fuss. He got the brilliant idea to toss one of these big uglies on my 12-year-old sister, Vickie Lynn. So he waited until she bent over and then he took a big green tobacco worm, about as long as Vickie's index finger and as fat around as a pencil, and threw it down the back of her shirt.

Instantly, she reared up like a wild pony and whacked him right across the face.

As Vickie Lynn later told me, "I was so fighting mad, they had to pull me off of him. Daddy had always told me that it was against the law to hit a white person, but I didn't think about that. I was mad."

As they were pulling Vickie Lynn off William, they threatened that the police were going to come to take her away.

William was speechless, but his bright red face said it all. His boyish prank had lit the short fuse of racial inequalities and he had no idea what to do about it.

He left quickly saying, "I have to hitch up another truck."

All eyes were on his grandmother. She was the only white person there. She was looping tobacco (tying leaves on to wooden poles for curing in the barns) with our momma. She could have called the police. As it was, she witnessed the mischief and decided to keep silent.

As Vickie Lynn stated so succinctly, "We were raised up to be afraid of white people."

But this created a bit of a conflict for the Gorham children because we were part white—more than most blacks with a heritage of slavery. During the slavery era, it was common for white masters to forcibly produce offspring with their black slave women. These children were considered black—regardless of how white their skin, hair, and facial features were, because they had one black parent. However, it was customary for the lighter offspring to work in the house, while the darker offspring worked in the fields.

In our case, I'm sure that some of the Gorham's experienced this racial mixing, but we also had something else. My mother's father, Mr. Jim Bundy, was a prominent and highly successful white businessman in Farmville, North Carolina, about 10 miles from Falkland. He was also a married man with two sons, Jim and Sam.

Mr. Jim Bundy owned the land that my Grandma Sarah Jordan and her husband, Milton Rasberry, sharecropped. Milton Raspberry died after fathering six children: Daisy, Lizzie, Calvin, Milton, Johnny, and Theodore. Somehow, a long-term romantic relationship developed between Grandma Sarah and Mr. Jim Bundy, resulting in 10 children that bore his likeness, but Grandma Sarah's maiden name Jordan. Their children were Annie Best, Walter, Malcolm, Jim, Glaster (fondly known as Uncle Puddin), Edward Thomas, the twins Sadie and Madie (my

momma born July 7, 1924), Susie Bea, and Wilbert.

Mr. Jim Bundy loved Grandma Sarah so well that he moved her to a two-story house near Joyner Crossroads, just outside of Farmville, and supported all 16 of her children. A few testaments to her lifestyle include a baby grand piano that graced her parlor, a Model T Ford that stayed in her driveway so that her son Theodore could drive wherever she pleased, and regular Sunday dinners to feed her entire church—Union Grove Baptist Church.

Even if Mr. Jim Bundy would have decided to divorce his white wife, in favor of marrying Grandma Sarah—law forbid it. In 1875, just 10 years after slavery was abolished, the state of North Carolina amended its constitution to read, "All marriages between a white person and a negro, or between a white person and a person of negro descent to the third generation inclusive are hereby forever prohibited." (Article 14, Section 8 NC Constitution 1875) In other words, it was a crime for blacks to marry whites.

North Carolina was so stubborn in its stance that even though the U.S. Supreme court declared laws prohibiting interracial marriages unconstitutional in 1967, it wasn't until 1971 that North Carolina amended its state constitution. Either way, even if it had not been against the legal precepts, it was certainly against the cultural norms—likely insuring social suicide for a white business leader.

However, Grandma Sarah didn't seem to have any trouble

with the color line. She was a very intelligent and attractive black woman with light "high yellow" skin that glowed like her warm personality. She was well respected by the black community and well loved by Mr. Jim Bundy. My Aunt Sadie, Momma's twin, told us that she used to watch her daddy (Mr. Jim Bundy) and her Momma take walks, hand in hand down the path at their homeplace.

Mr. Bundy was also a gentle and a genuine father to the children. He visited often, bringing gifts of candy or toys from town. He kept them outfitted in handsome clothing and spent time with them. When he was at their home, he was all theirs.

However, once he left their property—he was no longer their daddy. So when they came to Farmville—even though nine of his ten children could pass for white, with the exception of my Momma's twin, Sadie, he would not acknowledge them and they were forbidden to approach, nod, or even try to catch the eye of Mr. Jim Bundy.

Each child had to learn to navigate these tumultuous emotional waters for himself or herself. My momma, Madie Jordan Gorham, inherited skin as white as milk, silky red hair, bright green eyes, a sprinkling of freckles, and all the "white" facial features that go along with that. My momma could pass for white. In fact, she was so "white" that she could not pass for black.

After she and my daddy married, they were repeatedly pulled over by the police because it looked like a black man had

a white woman in the front seat with him. My parents had to constantly carry their birth certificates and marriage license to prove that they were both "black" and legally married according to law.

In fact, my daddy used to tell us a funny story about this. One night, he was driving Mr. W. W. Wooten's truck home from an out of town trip.

The police pulled him over and asked, "Whose truck are you driving?"

Daddy calmly and respectfully replied, "My boss man's, Sir."

The officer then shined the light on Momma and said, "And you have your boss man's wife with you too?"

Daddy said, "No sir. This is my wife."

Daddy had to get out his papers and "prove" to the officer that Momma was his wife.

It seems that from childhood, Momma found herself caught in a painful paradox. Sometimes, black children imagine that life would be better if they were white. At the time when Momma was growing up and even for most of my childhood, white children had better schools, more job opportunities, and top rung on the social hierarchy.

But being "white" did not make life easier for Momma. It actually made it more difficult. The white community in Farmville—who knew her origins shunned her, beginning with her own father when she was on his turf. And, while the black

community accepted her—she always had to "prove" she was black to anyone who had not previously met her.

So instead of making her stronger or more advantaged—being white actually gave her a bit of an inferiority complex. Whereas we, her children, knew "our place" in the world—even as it changed us and we changed it in the rapidly unfolding Civil Rights era—Momma never felt comfortable on either side of the color line.

SHARECROPPER'S WISDOM

Chapter 7

PAY NOW AND PLAY LATER

Click. Click. Click. Click.

Walt and I sat on the back of the tractor facing the rear. In front of each of us was a large basket holding hundreds of six to eight inch tobacco plants ready for transplanting.

Between us, an automated tobacco setter was mounted. At each "click," a metal hand flipped down "asking" for a plant. Quickly and carefully, one of us placed a plant in the hand—roots down and greens up—and then the next metal hand rotated into place begging for another plant.

Walt and I alternated. I'd feed the first hand, he'd feed

the next. Each time a hand rotated into place, an audible click could be heard.

"Come on, Walt," I said impatiently. "You gotta hit the click."

Walt was a year-and-a-half younger than me, but I showed him no mercy. He was an irritating little brother because before we were even in middle school, he had the nerve to grow bigger than me. But he wasn't faster!

Walt just rolled his eyes at me. Actually, he did a pretty good job hitting the click. He missed that time because he'd run out of plants and when he reached into the basket to get more, the roots were tangled.

No problem! Big brother saved the day. I got his click and my click too! But I let him know that it wasn't my job to hit his click.

"Next click is yours," I said sternly.

We settled into a nice easy rhythm. Click and set, click and set. James then Walt, James then Walt.

When I occasionally looked up, I could see a straight row of bright green tobacco plants growing one plant longer with each click. The tobacco setter placed them 24 inches apart and the machine did all the work. It leveled the top of the ground, dug a hole, placed the plant, and covered the roots. We even had a barrel of water strapped on to the front of the tractor to give each transplant a shot of water.

I realized that Walt and I had it easy compared to the

work our daddy did when he was a boy. Daddy had to plant thousands of tobacco plants by hand. He didn't get to sit on the back of a tractor hitting the click. He had to bend over, dig the hole, set the plant, and water—putting in about 7000 plants to the acre.

Worse yet, before planting, Daddy had to break up the ground using a mule and a single furrow plow. I got a taste of that when I was about seven. Even though I was a tiny little guy, probably weighing less than 50 pounds, Daddy decided to show me how to plow.

He took the rope from the mule, tied it in a knot, and placed in on the back of my neck.

Then he placed my hands on the plow and called to the mule, "Get up there, Gal."

When the mule stepped forward, I felt the tip of the plow sink into the earth and move forward. Immediately, the blade rolled a 10" swath of grass and weeds over, exposing the rich orange soil beneath. This swath, or trench, continued unbroken for the length of a football field. At the end of the row, Daddy turned the mule around and again we followed the plow, letting the mule do the brunt of the work. We only plowed a few rows, but as years passed, this single event left a fossil of a memory on the soft clay of my heart.

Feeling the power of the mule through the handles of the plow was fascinating and awe-inspiring. I was part of a team— accomplishing tremendous work. I was part of our annual

ritual—Daddy and I were breaking up the barren ground so this year's crops could grow.

Over time, I would come to appreciate that the way Daddy cared for the land—how he plowed, planted, fertilized, cultivated, and harvested—was directly related to how productive the land would be.

Likewise, Roy Gorham saw his mission as Daddy to do whatever it took to raise up his children to be as productive as possible in the soil of society. With that mission in mind, Daddy started my training—my planting, watering, and weeding—early in life.

Now part of my training took place in the field working side-by-side with Daddy. But, Daddy also gave me some responsibilities that I had to do on my own.

When I was about eight years old, it became my afterschool job to feed the hogs and the mules. Daddy assigned Walt to help me, but as the oldest, I was held accountable.

Daddy's only stipulation was that my work be done before dark. Now this wasn't too much of a problem in the early fall. It didn't get dark until 8 o'clock at night. So I could work on the farm, play with my friends, and buzz around on my bike—with plenty of time to feed the beasts.

However, in the wintertime, it grew dark by 6 o'clock. This created a problem because when I got off the bus, I wanted to reward myself with one cartoon before I fed the animals. So if the television in our house was working, I'd head in that

direction. If it was broken, I'd go next door to my little white neighbor friends, Pete and Danny Whitley.

The problem is: Cartoons are addictive. I'd watch one and then think that I had time to watch one more. I'd watch Bugs Bunny, Porky Pig, Roadrunner, Rocky and Bullwinkle, Huckleberry Hound, Mickey Mouse—they were endless and they were engaging. In fact, I made two promises to myself as a child. When I grew up, I would always watch cartoons and I would never wear shoes. Needless to say, I broke both promises!

Sometimes, even after the cartoons ended, I'd still be watching my favorite Westerns—the Lone Ranger or Maverick.

I'd be so mesmerized that Daddy could walk right in the room and I wouldn't even notice. Then, suddenly I'd feel a vicelike grip on the back of my neck. Daddy was driving me out the door saying, "Boy, didn't I tell you to get your work done before you watch TV? You get your work done first. Pay now and play later. You decided to play now and pay later. Now is later. It's time to pay."

It didn't matter if he'd caught me at home or in front of the neighbors TV, he'd start spanking me. I got the brunt of the beating and I only had to ask once why Walt didn't get in trouble as much as I did.

"You're older. You ought to know better," was Daddy's short reply.

As he continued to spank me, he would remind me that my beating was my choice. I could have done my work first. As

it was, I would still have to do my work, but I would also have to suffer a beating.

To this day, I don't know how Daddy knew that I didn't feed the animals. I don't know if he asked Momma—who may have told him that I stepped right off the bus and never budged from the television, or if he went to the barn every night to inspect my work. Whatever the case, Daddy was always right! He knew when I "forgot" either genuinely or on purpose.

Of course, after a beating, I would hold myself to paying now. But, it didn't take long for me to get distracted or overly optimistic about Daddy slipping up. Then, like most young boys, I'd decide that I was strong enough to watch just one cartoon and then do my chores. That rarely worked!

In reality, I should have known how important it was to feed the animals. I'd felt the power of the mule and knew that if I let Daddy's mules starve to death, we wouldn't be able to plow our fields. Also, I knew that the hogs supplied 90% of our meat. Aside from a few chickens, rabbits, squirrels, and fish—pork was the only meat on our table. Even at that, we did not have the luxury of eating meat every day.

Being irresponsible seemed to be the crabgrass of my youth. Just like Daddy tolerated no crabgrass or weeds around the base of his tobacco plants—because weeds sap the nutrients and invite pests—Daddy tolerated no irresponsibility in me.

It took years for me to learn this simple lesson: Either you can pay now and play later or you can play now and pay

later. But when I finally embraced this value, I found that it contained rare seeds for success.

Years later, when I was a student at East Carolina University, it was this quality that got me hired. I'd applied for a part-time job at a convenience store close to campus called Fast Fair. I'm sure they'd received hundreds of applications from college kids for countless years and they weren't too keen on hiring me.

Most college students like to P-A-R-T-Y more than they like to W-O-R-K. It's just part of the natural growth of a person. But these other students didn't have my daddy. He grew me up hard and quick, and that gave me an advantage.

When I determinedly went in for the seventh time asking for a job, the district manager asked me several times, "Do you really want a job in this store?"

I respectfully confirmed each time, "Yes Sir!"

He let me fill out an application. Then I thanked him and left.

At 7:30 that Friday night, just after I showered, dressed in my sharpest clothes, and prepared to step out and party—the phone rang. It was the district manager.

Once again he asked, "Do you really want a job in this store?"

I confirmed, "Yes sir!"

Then came the big question, "Are you prepared to come to work at 8 o'clock tonight? We will train you from 8 o'clock

to midnight and then that will be your shift."

So here I was. At the crossroads of pay now and play later or play now and pay later. I made the right choice and never missed a day of work. That led to new choices and you already know the rest of the story.

Chapter 8

YOU FOOLISH BOY

Daddy prided himself on being self-sufficient. He didn't have the money to run to the doctors for every little ache or pain, so mostly we used home cures.

Every winter, Daddy took a teaspoon of sugar, added two drops of kerosene and told us to swallow it. Then, he gave us a fresh slice of an orange to chase away the aftertaste. Daddy said this would kill any parasites we might have picked up in the summer.

Another home cure was tobacco. As a member of the St. John's Missionary Baptist Church, we could not use tobacco in any form for recreation. However, we did use it as medicine.

One day I was hoeing around the tobacco plants—chopping out the crabgrass—when a wasp stung me on my lip. I ran to Daddy.

Crying, I blubbered out, "Daddy, a wasp stung me."

Daddy could see it for himself. My lip swelled up like someone had punched me in the mouth.

Daddy looked at my lip, and without any pity or emotion at all said, "Go see Aunt Helen."

I ran over to his sister who was hoeing just a few rows over. Aunt Helen—who was not a member of our church—took one look at my lip, reached into her lower lip where she had a gooey wad of chewing tobacco, and then smeared some of the goo on my lips.

It was messy, but it worked. The stinging went away.

Nonetheless, I thought I deserved a break because I was injured, but that was not to be.

Daddy saw me heading for the shade and said, "Boy, get back to work."

It wasn't that he didn't care, but Daddy was not one to coddle his kids. I had a problem—a wasp sting—he fixed it. Sitting in the shade feeling sorry for myself wasn't going to help anyone.

It wasn't too long after that when I had a more serious incident. It was hog killing day, my favorite day of the year—not because I liked killing hogs, but because it was on this day that we ate our best meal of the year. It was better than Christmas,

better than Easter, better than any other day.

The day started at 6 a.m., which was typically the time we started our morning chores. Nothing was different except for the fact that I was a bit sleepy on this particular morning. So, I grabbed my smoked sausage sandwich in my right hand and headed down to the hog pen with my daddy.

When we arrived, Daddy gave me the knife, which I then held in my left hand. I knew that when my daddy called for the knife, I was to release my grip on the blade so that he could quickly cut the pig's throat and bleed it out.

For some reason, I wasn't really paying attention. I heard the "boom" when Daddy shot the pig in the head. And I heard Daddy say, "Okay, give me the knife."

But when I held out my hand, I forgot to open my fingers to release the blade. Daddy grabbed the knife and when he did, the expertly sharpened blade gashed open three of my fingers. As soon as the air hit the wounds, it began to sting.

I screamed out, "Daddy!"

He looked at my hand, blood gushing everywhere, and said, "You foolish boy! Come with me."

Needless to say, I was wide awake now. He marched me to the tobacco barn where we had a big drum of kerosene for curing the tobacco. He opened the valve and let kerosene run over my hand. The instant the kerosene touched my wounds, my fingers stopped hurting.

Then, Daddy took an old piece of cloth he found in the

barn—similar to gauze, but definitely not sterile—wrapped it around my hand, and tied it off. He once again shook his head and repeated, "Foolish boy," and then added, "Now, go on."

That was it. That was my First aide and actually my only aide. Nothing else was done. No stitches. No antibiotics. No doctor's visit. When the wrap came off a week later, my fingers were perfectly healed—barely leaving a ghost of a scar.

Incidentally, Daddy never apologized for this accident. He let me take full ownership. I'd been given instructions. I knew how to do my job. I wasn't paying attention, so I suffered the consequences. He was teaching me to bear my own load for my own actions.

Also—just like before—Daddy made me get back to work. After all, my pointer finger was unhurt on my left hand and my entire right hand worked just fine.

So I followed along as Daddy and two neighbor men carried the newly killed hog to the trough filled with boiling water. They carefully lowered the first hog—weighing about 300 pounds—into the water. I watched them use chains to roll the hog from side to side so that it would heat evenly.

Now the purpose of this hot bath is not to cook the pig, but to simply soften the hair. Until you see this for yourself, it's hard to believe how much hair pigs have. But once the hair begins to pull out easily, the adults work quickly, using a hog scraper—a specially designed metal disk on a short wooden handle—to quickly remove all the longer hairs.

Once that's done, it's time to get the pig out of the trough. So the men slit the back ankles and run a long pole through both ankles so that the pig can be hoisted up on a crossbeam. Before the next step, we usually had three pigs hanging up.

Now it's time for the close shave. Using extremely sharp knives, the men go over the entire pig until the skin is completely smooth and bare.

Then, they remove the intestines. That's when I stopped watching and started working. When I was 9 years old, it became my job to process the intestines. It may make you squeamish to read about this, but I had to actually do it!

First, I'd use a hole digger—kind of like two shovels bolted together—to chomp out one bite of dirt at a time until I had a hole about as big around as a basketball and about three feet deep.

Next, I went to the creek and cut five reeds. I cut one end of the reed at an angle so that it had a point on it. I set the reeds aside and went to get the intestines. I cut the intestines into four-foot lengths. Then I placed one end of the intestine in the hole, while pouring hot water down the top of the other end. The hot water loosened the feces, and eventually it slid out into the bottom of the hole.

I rinsed the section of intestine with hot water several times until all of the solids were flushed out. Then I pierced one end of the intestine with the tip of my reed, and pushed the entire length of the intestine over the top of my reed. After that,

I simply had to pick up the end of the intestine that was stuck on my reed, pull it out, and the whole intestine turned inside out in an instant.

Now it was time for the good cleaning. We built a fire under a large iron pot—about 18" from side to side if you cross through the middle—that sat right on the coals. Once the water started boiling, I dropped in the intestines and stirred them with a stick. I repeated this four times to make sure that I really got them clean.

Momma did the final cleaning and then they were ready to use. While I'd been doing my job, Momma and two neighbor women mixed the ingredients for sausage. Once it was ready, it was my job to fill the casings (intestines) with the sausage meat.

We had a little machine that made this easy and it was actually kind of fun. I slid the casing on to a little groove on the machine that held the casing in place. Then I turned a handle, and the meat was forced into the casing. About every 18 inches, I cut the casing and tied the ends and the middle with twine. Then we hung the sausages in the smoke house.

I stuffed the pig's stomach—believe it or not—with sausage the same way. When it's full, it's about half the size of a softball. We always called it a Tom Thumb, but it's also known as a dandoodle sausage and yes, as of the year 2016, you can still buy these in North Carolina!

It's probably apparent by now, that sharecroppers used every single part of the pig. We ate all the tradition cuts, such

as the hams, chops, ribs, loins, and bacon—although ours was about three times as thick as what you typically buy at the grocery store.

We also ate the heart, liver, kidneys, skin (pork rinds) and my favorite—the tongue. I also liked the ears, the feet, and my absolute favorite was stewed chittlins (small intestines). Daddy's favorite was the brains, which he scrambled with eggs. In fact, it was a New Year's tradition to serve hog's head.

The women also "render the fat." Basically, the fat—sometimes over 30 pounds on a pig—is ground up and cooked in that same iron pot outside at a very low temperature. As it melts, tiny pieces of meat fall to the bottom. Then, the hot liquid fat is strained and stored in mason jars or cans. When it's cooled, it becomes a white solid known as lard.

Momma used this lard all year long to make biscuits, fry eggs, and on a rare good day, to make sweet potato pie. Oh, and the little bits of meat that fell to the bottom—those are called cracklings—and they are delicious!

We all worked hard—sometimes processing two to four hogs—until about 7 o'clock that evening. Then, we all shared in the reward. The hosting family spread a virtual feast for all who came and helped. We had fresh fried tenderloin—the most tender cut of pork— and a rare "all you can eat" spread of sweet potatoes, white potatoes, cabbage, collard greens, butter beans, hot corn bread, and biscuits smothered in sweet molasses! Mmm. Mmm. Mmm!

SHARECROPPER'S WISDOM

Chapter 9

LORD, I STRETCH MY HAND TO THEE

We didn't argue with Daddy...ever! We were raised in a small, isolated community that supported the same values that Daddy taught. The outside world had very little influence on us. So, when the rest of America began it's "counterculture" movement in 1964—rebelling against parents, rejecting materialism, and turning inward to "find oneself"—we continued in our "old-fashioned" values.

In medical terms, you might call this "herd immunity." In other words, because virtually all of our peers had been vaccinated with an unquestioning respect for parents, a high regard for school and church, and an outward turning to serve

others, the social virus of rebellion could not find enough "unprotected" youth to start an outbreak in the black community in Falkland.

However, the Gorham family did play a key role in the advancement of Civil Rights—fair and equal treatment of all people regardless of skin color—in our community. This was no rebellion. It was an organized call to leadership, which required self-sacrifice, obedience, commitment, and endurance. In our family, it all began with Daddy.

Prior to the 1960s, it was very difficult for a black man to gain a position of authority in his community. In fact, there were only two areas where most men could hope to lead—in his own home and in his church. At St. John's Missionary Baptist Church, a man first had to prove he could lead in his home before he would ever be considered for appointment as a deacon (a leader who helped the Pastor) in the church.

Of course, you're not a leader if you don't have followers, and Daddy's first willing follower needed to be his wife. As head of household, Daddy needed to win the support and respect of Momma.

Daddy made that easy for Momma. He worked hard to provide and even did much of the outdoor farm work that wives typically help with because Momma was so pale that she couldn't tan.

He also told Momma to direct the children to him when there were decisions to be made. Momma was happy to comply.

When I wanted to go someplace or do something, it was simply no use to ask Momma.

Every time, Momma would say, "Go ask your Daddy."

Momma didn't cross Daddy in front of us children or in public. But, I know for certain that she didn't always agree with him. I remember many a night when Big Man Jones, or another drunk, would end up on our porch at 3 o'clock in the morning.

"Roy," Big Man would moan, "take me home."

He'd keep it up until Daddy would roll out of bed. While Daddy was putting on his clothes, I'd hear Momma protest. I couldn't help but hear, because when you live in a four-room house with no insulation, you hear everything!

"Roy, you ain't nothin but a fool. That's why he keeps coming up here, because he knows that you are going to get up and drive him home."

Daddy would calmly say, "Madie, it's the right thing to do."

Momma would counter angrily, "If you'd stop taking these drunks home, then maybe they'd stop coming up here. We have all these other people in the community. Why do you think they only come to you? Because they know you will get up and take them home."

Instead of repaying anger with anger, Daddy simply turned the other cheek and kindly repeated, "Madie, it's the right thing to do."

It didn't matter if it was below freezing, raining, or

snowing, Daddy would leave his warm bed and drive a man home that most people had judged as "unworthy."

In his action, Daddy taught me how to honor a wife without compromising your own values. And, Daddy taught me the manly art of compassion.

He also modeled to the rest of the community—church family or otherwise—that they could count on Daddy for help even if they didn't "deserve" it. Even the white folks noticed Daddy's unswerving adherence to Jesus' Golden Rule: "So whatever you wish that others would do to you, do also to them."

As our leader, Daddy protected his children fiercely. He limited our outside influences to three arenas. We could go to school, go to church, and go to visit family. Part of this was due to our limited finances, but mainly it was because Daddy wanted to keep us safe.

He was actually much stricter with his first five children—all girls. He would not let them stay home alone. Midweek, when Momma and Daddy went to a prayer meeting, the girls had to go along, and do their homework there.

Joyce C., the oldest, once asked Daddy, "Why can't we do our homework at home?"

Daddy understood the inclinations of youth.

He lovingly told her, "I have five pretty daughters and I want them to stay that way."

When my sisters came of age to date, Daddy was right there. It's a wonder any of them got married. Daddy made the

boys come to our house and sit in our living room. Then, we all sat there and watched them.

Daddy had us so well trained—we wanted his approval and feared his discipline—that the church noticed. About six years after Daddy joined the church and turned his life around, he was deemed to be presiding over his household in a fine manner.

The church also noticed that Daddy comforted the sick, reached out to the orphans and widows, and supported the church by tithing (freely giving 10% of his earnings), cleaning the building, and coming early to light the fire in the wood stove.

It got to the point where everyone thought Daddy was already a Deacon. And that is the way it is done at St. John's Missionary Baptist Church. The mantle of authority is not put on a man with the expectation that he will grow into it. It is bestowed upon the man who is already measuring up.

Daddy was ordained as a Deacon in 1962, when I was six years old. I remember the day clearly. He was called upon to lead the congregation in prayer. Daddy humbly got down on one knee, stretched his hand heavenward and prayed, "Lord, I stretch my hand to Thee. No other help do I know. If you remove yourself from me Lord, whither shall I go?"

He flowed seamlessly into a heartfelt prayer, sometimes clapping to create a rhythm or to punctuate a point. When the service concluded, the whole congregation embraced him. It was time. It was the right thing to do, to ordain Daddy as a

Deacon.

From that point forward, Daddy used the first verse of this hymn (Father, I Stretch My Hand to Thee) written by Charles Wesley in the 1700s to open his prayers.

Daddy's ordination validated his role as a community leader and this opened new doors of leadership. St. John's Missionary Baptist Church was a member of the Middle Eastern District—which networked regional Baptist churches—meeting every three months at designated churches. The Middle Eastern District in turn received national support.

Also, Daddy became active in the local chapter of the NAACP (National Association for the Advancement of Colored People), which met 10 miles away in Greenville.

According to the official website of the NC NAACP: "The NAACP's mission has remained constant for its first century: to ensure the political, educational, social, and economic equality of rights of ALL PERSONS (caps mine) and to eliminate racial hatred and racial discrimination."

Everything Daddy learned at the NAACP, he brought back to the church—which was the social hub of the black community. In turn, he took concerns of the church members with him to the NAACP meetings. Daddy, along with his best friend and fellow Deacon Charlie Dupree and other church leaders, helped maintain a very vibrant and free flowing communication network that allowed national news and Civil Rights strategies to be understood and interpreted, giving the black community of

Falkland and all of Pitt County the ability to act as one united body.

Networks like this were established across the United States—uniting the black community more tightly than probably any other segment of the population. With changes in the political system, Daddy knew the season was quickly approaching to take personal action in the name of Civil Rights in Falkland.

St. John Baptist Church, Falkland, NC

SHARECROPPER'S WISDOM

Chapter 10

IF YOU HANG AROUND LONG ENOUGH

Daddy only completed the seventh grade in school. But, he added to his knowledge and wisdom daily. Every day he went to work in the fields, he was learning in God's classroom.

One personal value Daddy learned was patience. Even the best seeds in the best soil take time to grow. But when it came to Civil Rights—changing the attitudes of all people about the fair treatment of people of color—Daddy knew that the soil of the nation was hard as a rock.

He'd cleared land as a boy and knew that it took mighty effort to chop down the big trees and surly underbrush—just

to clear the land. Even then—when the visible obstacles were removed—underground roots held the soil compactly together. It's actually harder work to remove the hidden roots than it is to topple the tree. And lastly, the field has to be plowed and leveled to be ready for planting.

Social reform was no different. The big trees of segregation—often known as the Jim Crow laws—had to be toppled. These state and local laws had been growing since the 1800s, having been carefully crafted, rooted, and nurtured in the Southern states after the abolition of slavery.

When the first big tree was toppled in 1954, in the landmark United States Supreme Court Case Brown vs. Board of Education of Topeka, declaring separate public schools for blacks and whites to be unconstitutional—Daddy had his oldest two daughters, Joyce C. and Lillie Gray attending school at Bruce Falkland Elementary.

In North Carolina—a Southern state—it was against the law for his children to attend the white school—Falkland Elementary. Daddy knew that just as the Supreme Court declared, "separate educational facilities are inherently unequal."

However, Daddy didn't try to force the issue. Instead, he waited patiently and followed the news. One bright hope on the horizon was a white man who was born two years before Daddy. He was a fighter—serving in the millitary just like Daddy—and had overcome a few tough obstacles in his own rights by becoming the youngest man to ever become President

of the United States and the only Catholic to date. He was none other than John F. Kennedy.

In 1960, while running for office, Senator Kennedy verbally supported Civil Rights for all, and even, with the help of his younger brother, Robert Kennedy, secured the release of black Baptist minister and activist, Martin Luther King, Jr., from jail in Georgia.

Martin Luther King, Jr., was born in 1929, ten years after Daddy. He was a fighter too. In 1955, he led the Montgomery Bus Boycott after Rosa Parks refused to give up her bus seat to a white man. Four days later, Martin Luther King, Jr., was instrumental in organizing a 381-day boycott of city buses by blacks. This culminated in a U.S. Supreme Court mandate that Montgomery, Alabama integrate (open all seats for everyone) their bus system. This victory launched Martin Luther King, Jr., into the national spotlight as a civil rights activist.

Then, in 1960, when it became known that Martin Luther King, Jr., had the attention and support of presidential candidate, John F. Kennedy—Daddy and all the blacks in the "network" knew that the time and the season truly was changing.

By this time, Daddy had all five girls at Bruce Falkland Elementary School—which actually served grades first through eighth. Still, Daddy remained patient as sit-ins, marches, and other non-violent demonstrations cut into the compacted soil of the American conscience and readied the community for action in Falkland.

One reason for the slower than molasses progress in Civil Rights was that people tended to see it as a local (Southern) or legal problem. The average American did not see a reason to get behind the progress.

Here is where President John F. Kennedy made his biggest contribution. He helped the country reframe the problem of "unequal rights" as a moral issue. In his June 11, 1963 Civil Rights Address he said, "We are confronted primarily with a moral issue.... It is as old as the scriptures and is as clear as the American Constitution.... One hundred years of delay have passed since President Lincoln freed the slaves, yet their heirs... are not fully free. They are not yet freed from the bonds of injustice... this Nation... will not be fully free until all its citizens are free.... Now the time has come for this Nation to fulfill its promise."

The black community in Falkland was elated when the President then rolled out his plans to make it illegal to discriminate in public places—like schools, buses, and lunch counters—and in employment and programs funded by the federal government. Then, the unthinkable happened. President John F. Kennedy was assassinated on November 22, 1963, before he could sign his proposal into law.

My sister, Sarah Elizabeth, was sitting in her 7th grade social studies class when she heard the news.

She recently told me, "Principal Monk came in and whispered the news into my teacher's ear. I overheard it and

was so shocked that I kept staring at his shoes. I would not move my eyes from his shoes because I believed that if I did, what he said would be true."

When Ms. Viola Vines announced the news to her class—making it official—my sister had a physical reaction. She felt a lump come up in her throat that refused to leave for two weeks.

Sarah said, "Ms. Vines told us, 'Pay attention to everything you see, because you are watching history be made. One day you will tell other people about it.'"

Sarah said that she saw the whole country collapse. John F. Kennedy was not just a hero in the black community—but in the entire nation.

However, even death could not stop the progress now. The seed of Civil Rights finally geminated when the political and legal will united with the moral conscience of Americans. What resulted was the passage of the Civil Rights Act of 1964, on July 2.

Daddy always said, "Life is like the weather. If you hang around long enough, sooner or later it's going to change." The sun was finally shining on integration.

SHARECROPPER'S WISDOM

Chapter 11

IT'S THE RIGHT THING TO DO

The black community in Falkland—in the schools, in the church, and in the streets—was excited about the doors of opportunity afforded by the Civil Rights Act of 1964. However, they were also realistic.

Our family and every other family knew—either by the network or the national news—that people leading change were often jailed, slandered, physically attacked, or even murdered. So the black community of Falkland was not 100% for integrating the schools. Just for the record, the white community was nearly 100% against it.

One person who fanned the flames of change was the daughter of Deacon Charlie Dupree—Norice. By the time the

Civil Rights Act of 1964 was signed into law, Norice Dupree had already graduated from North Carolina A & T State University—one of the oldest historically black colleges in the United States.

In fact, it was four freshmen from NC A & T that sparked the civil rights movement in Greensboro, NC on February 1, 1960 by their "sit in" at the Woolworth's lunch counter. When city leaders asked the university to control its students and keep them on campus, President Warmoth T. Gibbs replied, "We teach our students how to think, not what to think."

That is the soil that Norice had been growing in for four years and she brought her activism back to little Falkland when she moved home and took a teaching job at Grimesland Elementary School, outside of Greenville.

She was a driving force in the local NAACP and with her connections from NC A & T, she actually arranged for my daddy and her daddy to meet Dr. Martin Luther King, Jr., in Edenton, North Carolina. Unfortunately, this is one of the tours that Dr. King canceled, so the meeting never took place.

However, what did take place was a united effort by our schools, our churches (Falkland actually had two black churches), and the NAACP to integrate the white high school serving Falkland at the earliest opportunity. That opportunity came in 1965. And who would believe that all four of the girls who would willingly transplant themselves in the resistant soil of Farmville High School would come from the tiny seedbed

of Falkland. One of those transplants was my sister, Sarah Elizabeth.

Now I was only 9 years old at the time and frankly, I didn't know or particularly care to know what was going on. So I'm going to let my sister, Sarah tell how she and Daddy—along with a handful of others—plowed up the fields of conformity, complacency, and criticism to make it easier for the rest of us who followed.

Below is Sarah Elizabeth's story.

I've loved and collected words my whole life. So when I was six-years old and had memorized the Pledge of Allegiance at school, I really thought about what it meant.

I pledge Allegiance to the flag
of the United States of America
and to the Republic for which it stands,
one nation under God, indivisible,
with Liberty and Justice for all.

That same year, I had to be hospitalized. When we arrived, I noticed that one sign said "white" and the other sign said "colored." We had to go to the colored section.

That opened my eyes and I began seeing the signs everywhere. I saw them in the department stores—and noticed the unequal treatment. If Daddy and I were being waited on and a white customer suddenly came in—Daddy was abandoned

until the white person was served.

When we went to a restaurant—the sign said we had to place our order at the back of the store, while the white person got the royal treatment. Whites were invited to walk in the front door, sit at nice tables, and be served like welcomed guests.

It wasn't too long before I realized that what the pledge said about being ONE nation and having LIBERTY and JUSTICE for ALL—it wasn't true. It wasn't true for black Americans. So I always had my eyes open for ways to make it true.

At church, I'd hear my teachers talking to the Deacons, complaining that the white schools had better books and better resources. I loved books and I loved school. I wanted that for myself.

By middle school, I was reading the local newspapers and watching televised news to track the civil rights movement. This was a personal mission of mine—not forced upon me by anyone.

Also, Reverend O. J. Rooks, who was active in the NAACP and in charge of the local Baptist Training Union, brought with him the latest news about the civil rights when he met with youth from 22 local churches every three months. He taught us the principles of non-violence as a way to lead change and helped us follow the leadership of Martin Luther King, Jr.

He also introduced us to the Black Panthers—a group that used violence to demand equality—and while he forbid us from imitating their behavior, we secretly held them as heroes.

On top of all of this, I was best friends with Norice Dupree's little sister, Minerva. Minerva was not only immersed in the same steady stream of civil rights media that I enjoyed—she actually lived with the local fountainhead of proactive ideas.

So when I completed 9th grade at the black high school—H. B. Suggs—and my teachers asked me to be one of the first students to integrate Farmville High School, I heard the same little voice in my head that I'd heard from my Daddy's lips many times,

"It's the right thing to do."

But it wasn't Daddy's voice speaking to me. It was my own voice. I knew that for me—Sarah Elizabeth Gorham—this was the mission that I was born for.

I didn't need my teachers to remind me that I was a top student, involved in every club, well-liked by my fellow students, and having all indications that I would have the strength, fortitude, and commitment to see this decision through.

I wanted it for me. I wanted the better books. I wanted the better resources. And I wanted to be a part of the change that was happening in the country so that the Pledge of Allegiance would finally be true.

On all counts—it was the right thing for me to do.

SHARECROPPER'S WISDOM

Chapter 12

LORD, DISPATCH YOUR ANGELS

S arah Elizabeth's story continues below:
 I signed the enrollment application for Farmville High School before I even talked to Daddy. Then, almost immediately, I regretted it. I was popular at school and figured that my friends would follow my lead and lots of us would attend the white school. But, that was not to be.

Even my own sisters, Madie Sue and Lillie Gray, told me that I was crazy. They asked, "Why would you want to go to a school where you are not wanted?"

In town, there were murmurings that if black students from Falkland integrated the white school in Farmville, it might invite cross burnings, home burnings, or even murder by the Klu

Klux Klan.

Sharecroppers—who depended on white landowners for their homes and their employment—feared that the bold action of a few might jeopardize the livelihood of all.

That sealed it for me. The more I heard against it, the more determined I was to do it. I felt that if I did not take action—now that the law allowed it—then all the peaceful marches I'd participated in and all the sermons that I'd listened to would have been for naught.

I wanted to be like Dr. Martin Luther King, Jr. When I watched him on television, I didn't hear his words. Black people had been talking for decades about equality. So I wasn't interested in his words.

I saw his courage. That is what I wanted in my life. He didn't talk about marches, he led them. He did it even though he KNEW that he would be arrested and put in jail. This man actually went and DID what he told other people to do. And he did it KNOWING in advance that he was going to be treated badly.

Integration was no longer about better books or better schools for me. It was about doing my part to bring about equal treatment for people of all colors. I saw it as something I needed to do for Falkland.

My teachers, Mrs. Armistead and Mr. Michael Vick, had assured me, "You can do it." I purged my heart and mind of any doubts and decided, "I will do it." After all, if not me, then

who?

When I showed Daddy the application, he and Momma signed it. They didn't encourage me and they didn't shut me down. It had to be my choice.

Daddy figured that if any of his children could break the color barrier, it would be me. Daddy always called me "fast." He wasn't talking about my speed or intellect. He was talking about my nature. Fast is a nice way of saying aggressive and I would need to be emotionally aggressive to bear the insults that shortly lay ahead of me without resorting to breakdown or blow up.

As it turned out, four of us attended Farmville High School in the fall of 1965. Minerva Dupree and I were just entering the 10th grade. We shared a lot in common. Our daddies were best friends and so were we. We were neighbors, sharecroppers, active in the church, but Minerva's dad had a seasonal job at DuPont, so they were a little more affluent than we were.

The other two girls were the daughters of educators and much more affluent than us. Gwendolyn Graves, who also enrolled as a sophomore, was the daughter of a third grade teacher and her father worked out of state.

Beverly Monk, who enrolled as a junior, was the daughter of Gaston Monk, the Principal of Bruce Falkland Elementary School. Her mom, Virginia Mills Monk, was a teacher at our school. Gaston Monk was also very involved in the Pitt County

NAACP, serving as its president.

The four of us received special training and coaching from the NAACP throughout the summer of 1965 to prepare us for our task. We were told that at all times we were to remain non-violent. If we were attacked, we were to try to escape. But if we could not, then we were to cover our heads and lay down on the ground.

If we were insulted, we were advised to ignore it or to smile. This was in line with the old adage to "Kill them with kindness."

We were reminded that someone had to be the first and that by our courage, we would smooth the way for our younger brothers and sisters, our future children, and our grandchildren. Incidentally, before we stepped into Farmville High School, Principal Sam D. Bundy stepped down. We are not sure why he decided to become principal of the elementary school—which would later be named in his honor—but we suspect that he did not want to draw attention to the fact that one of his father's "black" grandchildren was spearheading the integration.

Nothing could have prepared us for that first day. Daddy drove me to school because the Board of Education would not allow us to ride the bus to the white school. In hindsight, this was probably a blessing. Before dropping me off, Daddy said a prayer with me.

Daddy pleaded, "Lord, dispatch your angels to keep Sarah safe."

Then, Daddy dropped me off in front of the school and pulled across the street to the city bus station to watch. Everybody knew what was happening—four black girls were stepping foot into Farmville High School for the first time. Whites and blacks alike were driving up and down the road, craning their necks to see if there would be an incident.

When the whites drove by, they honked their horns in protest and screamed out the window, "Niggers!" or "Go back to where you belong!" or "We don't want you!"

Finally, the school doors opened and the four of us went inside. The students acted no better than the adults did. We were blasted with a relentless barrage of insults.

We were called "Aunt Jemima"—implying that a black woman's place is to be a Mammy—someone who nursed white people's babies, cooked for the family, and cleaned their toilets.

We were called "Tar-Baby"—the Uncle Remus character that looks like a real person but was really nothing but a brainless, heartless lump of black tar with clothes on.

Mostly, we were called "Nigger"—one of the most offensive racist words carrying a sense of contempt, ignorance, and enslavement.

As we made it to our classes—the teachers ignored the students' hateful behavior. I interpreted their silence as consent.

I thought it would be better when we finally got to class, because in the black schools, the teachers always protected the students. But that wasn't the case at Farmville High School.

Most of the teachers barely tolerated our presence. Some of them blatantly scorned us.

When I walked into each classroom—everyone stood up until I picked my seat. No one wanted to sit next to a black girl. When I walked between the desks, students stuck out their feet to try to trip me.

On my first day in math class, the teacher asked me to come to the board to solve a math problem. I think she wanted to publicly humiliate me. Math is not my strong suit, but thankfully, I did the problem correctly.

Her response: "Oh, so you a smart one." She was implying that most blacks are stupid and I was the exception to the rule.

All of this set the stage for what I would experience for the next three years. Every day, I would be insulted, isolated, and targeted.

So for the next three years, I went to school scared, with a stomachache every single day. To make matters worse, I couldn't tell Momma and Daddy what was going on or they would have taken me out of that school.

I didn't want that. I'd given my word and I wanted to keep my word. I felt like I was carrying the world on my shoulders and I didn't want to feel the guilt if I let my community down. So I continued.

By working with my church leaders and mentors at the NAACP on a weekly basis, I was able to recover enough

to keep going the following week. Moreover, every week that I survived—was a victory for Civil Rights. Integrating schools was happening all over North Carolina and in other Southern States, and together we really were making a difference.

In social studies class, the teacher always singled out the student with the highest grade. One week, he didn't call out the name. The class kept asking, "Who got the highest grade?" He wouldn't answer. Finally, they badgered him so much that he threw my paper on my desk and said, "That gal over there."

I'll never forget that because at my house, a "gal" was a mule. Now, whether he was calling me a Jackass or not—he still refused to honor me by using my proper name. I felt so humiliated because I'd worked so hard to earn that grade.

The only extracurricular activity that I joined was the marching band. I played the bell lyre—similar to the xylophone. We performed every Friday night, home or away. I remember the first time I stepped on to the bus, everyone else got off. They refused to ride on the bus with me.

The thought crossed my mind, "Wow! I have the power to clear a bus!"

To save the day, my teacher let me ride with him and his wife to all the games for three years. Interestingly, two of the other black girls—Gwendolyn and Beverly—were also in band. Their parents could afford to buy them a car and they drove to the games. I didn't ride with them because we didn't travel in the same circles.

The longer I stayed at Farmville High School, the more I found the words of German philosopher, Friedrich Nietzsche, to be true: "What doesn't kill you makes you stronger."

I discovered a growing inner strength that comes from standing up for your rights—no matter the cost. This emboldened me to seek out new ways to challenge the social norms when I was away from school.

For instance—I used to put on my official Farmville High School band uniform and then purposely go into stores and public buildings. People's first reaction was that a black girl does not belong in a white school's uniform. But I was there to show them that I did. I was turning into a real rebel!

Someone told Daddy, "Someone is going to shoot Sarah if she wears that uniform."

They never shot me. In fact, in my three years at Farmville High School, I can say that I never experienced any physical violence. The closest anyone came to harming me was the boys who smoked.

At that time, they were allowed to bring their matches and cigarettes to school. When the teachers weren't looking, they would light a match and threaten to burn my long black hair. They did light the match, but they never burned my hair.

With the daily downpour of insults and threats—I have to say that I never caved in. I never let them see me cry and I never returned evil for evil. However, every day was a struggle.

One teacher in particular seemed to outright hate me.

She blatantly disrespected me and let the students in her class berate me.

She was my chemistry teacher and she would say, "You are the dumbest thing I've ever seen."

She was determined to fail me. However, she had a student teacher from East Carolina University—a white male about 21 years old—and he was equally determined to pass me. He worked with me and I passed the class.

SHARECROPPER'S WISDOM

Chapter 13

BE DEPENDABLE

S*arah's story continues: My toughest day happened the month before I graduated. On April 4, 1968, Dr. Martin Luther King, Jr., was assassinated. The next day, when Minerva and I walked into the school—everyone was cheering and celebrating.*

I remember standing in the school foyer—devastated! That was the first time that I thought, "Everything that I've fought for over the past three years is for naught because Martin Luther King was dead."

Our English teacher, Mr. Lawrence, walked into his class to find everyone celebrating King's murder. He looked at Minerva and I and then ordered, "Everyone sit down and write

your feelings."

He did that for Minerva and me. He did that to stop the heartless mockery. As I began to write, all the rage that I'd suppressed from all the pain and suffering found a voice. I was so hurt and so shocked. It was all that I could do to keep from crying.

I thought, "If they could kill Martin Luther King, they could kill me."

I felt lost and said to myself, "Who will tell us what to do? Who will take his place? Will things go back to the way they were before? We stepped forward and now we have stepped backward. All this time there was one person giving good directions nationwide. Then, he was cut down and so viciously."

A few days later, the black high school—HB Suggs— planned a march in honor of Dr. King. Momma sent a note to our principal at Farmville High School to get permission for me to be excused from school to join in the march. Permission was denied.

Momma—who typically avoided confrontation—got on the phone and talked to the Principal. Permission was granted.

Local ministers and teachers led us on a march down Main Street in Farmville between the black high school and the white high school. When I was walking, I felt sad. I wanted to cry. I felt angry. I think that all the anger I'd been holding in those three years had rushed to the surface, and for the first time in my life, I wanted to hit someone.

I wanted someone else to suffer the pain. Those cheering students, those mocking students at Farmville High School needed to feel the pain that I felt.

This happened so close to graduation—only a month away—that I decided that I had to finish this.

At the same time, I was one of the first black employees to work at Hollowell Drug Store in Greenville. I started working there after school and on weekends when I was 16. So I would go to school and battle the insults all day long, only to then go to work in a drug store where most people in the community only wanted to do business with white people.

The NAACP had petitioned businesses to employ black students and my sister, Joyce C., was actually the first one to lead the way at Hollowell Drug Store. She worked there a short time before she graduated. She had such an excellent work ethic that when she moved to Washington, D.C., they hired me.

I started out at the counter like everyone else, making milk shakes and egg salad sandwiches. But customers didn't always treat me like the white clerks.

When I asked for their order, some white folks would refuse to talk to me, as if I was invisible. Others were more straightforward. They would say, "I don't want your black hands touching my food."

Sometimes, if I was on the far right of the counter, I would see them purposely move to the far left. That was a signal, "I don't want you." I simply stepped back and let someone else

help them.

That first year was the hardest. After that, more and more blacks were working in the local businesses and that made it easier for everyone.

The next year at Hollowell's, I was transferred to the make-up counter. That was easier for the customers, and my fellow workers loved working with me. I would work anytime that I could. So when the other girls had dates, they knew that they could count on me to take their shift. I didn't have any dates. I was looked at like I had the plague—even by the black boys. No one was sure how my bold stand at Farmville or at work was going to pan out. They all had a wait and see attitude.

In the meantime, I loved working. For the first time in my life, I had money in my pocket and I went shopping every weekend. Mr. Hollowell loved my work ethic. Daddy raised us up to be superworkers. In fact, before I accepted the job, Daddy's brief advice to me was, "Be dependable."

We kept ourselves busy at all times—cleaning, stocking, organizing, and anticipating. Mr. Hollowell knew who was working and who was sloughing off, because he watched us from his glass window from up top in the pharmacy.

When I was a senior, I was promoted to working with the drugs and my relationship with the customers eased considerably. This was for two reasons. First, everyone knew that if you were working with drugs, you were a trusted worker. Second, people don't complain when you are handing them their medicine. It's

a whole different thing, giving someone medicine versus giving someone an ice cream cone.

In time, more blacks were employed at Hollowell's. My future brother-in-law, Donnie Phillips—who married my little sister Vickie Lynn—was hired to make deliveries along with a black man named CJ.

In all of this—when I was at work or at school—Daddy did his part to keep me safe. The first year, he and Charlie Dupree took turns driving me and Minerva, each offering daily prayers for our safety. Then, these two black men had the courage to challenge the Board of Education and we were finally allowed to ride the black bus, while being dropped at the white high school.

When it came to work, Daddy personally drove me to Hollowell Drug Store and watched me go in the door. Then, he came to pick me up an hour and a half before my shift ended. He always parked directly in front of the door, came in to buy an ice cream to let me know he was there, and then waited in the car until I came out.

Through all of this—I feel that my leadership in integrating the white school and being one of the first black employees at Hollowell Drug Store liberated Daddy. By extension, it let Roy "Joy" Gorham see the fruition of a dream that he had so patiently prepared for!

The next leader to come up in our family was Vickie Lynn. She chose to go to Farmville High School as a freshman. She's three years younger than me and she was the only black

student in her class, whereas I had Minerva and Gwendolyn as classmates.

Vickie Lynn told me that she chose Farmville because she wanted to follow in my footsteps and she wanted to play basketball. She had a very complex relationship with her fellow students. During basketball season, when she won virtually every trophy and recognition, she was treated with respect. But as soon as the season ended, the students treated her with contempt—mocking, insulting, and disrespecting her.

She told me, "Once the season was over, my teammates went along with the crowd. The same people who were applauding me a month earlier were now saying, 'You're not smart enough to be here.'"

Vickie Lynn had actually graduated salutatorian of her 8th grade class. However, with all the mocking by her classmates and her teachers refusing to call on her when she raised her hand, she shut down.

She told me, "My skin tone and hair color was similar to theirs, but they looked down on me because I had black blood in me. But if I had to do it over again, I would do it the same way because even though my grades suffered, it made me a stronger person."

Vickie Lynn never told us how rough she had it when we were young. Only recently did she tell me that, like me, she never told Daddy or anyone else how afraid she was. She didn't want to be told to quit.

Instead, she told it all to Jesus. She told me, "I called Jesus my imaginary friend. I felt like he was with me all the way. I prayed that these people would one day accept me for who I am."

By the time Vickie Lynn graduated in 1971, Farmville High School was completely integrated. So when my little brother, James, was ready for high school—all the students were going to Farmville High School. But I'll let him tell his story in a later chapter.

Meantime, after graduation, I—Sarah Elizabeth Gorham—had my sights set on becoming a teacher, but I didn't have any money for college. A black doctor in Greenville— A.A. Best, M.D.—sponsored my education. After earning my bachelors of English at Fayetteville State University, I became one of the first black teachers at Milton M. Sommer's Middle School in La Plata, Maryland.

I took all the lessons I learned from my first nine teachers and I became all of them in one. I brought song into my 6th grade classroom, discipline, humor, belief in children, good manners, initiative, proper dress, a sense of history, and leadership.

I also knew what not to do—lessons I learned at Farmville High School. Never judge students by the way they look, never allow students to bully classmates, and never humiliate a child.

By using that recipe, the students actually wanted to be in my class. They looked forward to our time together. And just like Ms. Viola Vines told me, I always told my students, "Pay

attention to everything you see, because you are watching history be made. One day you will tell other people about it."

In 2006, after 35 years of teaching 6th grade English, I was named Charles County Teacher of the Year. Each of those years, I shared my stories of growing up with a daddy who believed that values were more important than money. I told the children how I helped integrate Farmville High School. And I showed the children the indelible mark that President John F. Kennedy, Dr. Martin Luther King, Jr., and Presidential Candidate Robert F. Kennedy left on my heart.

*Sarah receiving
Teacher of the Year award.*

Chapter 14

KNOW THE DIFFERENCE
BETWEEN A NEED AND A WANT

Daddy kept a tight rein on his children. He'd sooner let a mule wander aimlessly through a newly planted field, than to let his children hang out with their friends and roam about town. And, we knew that wasn't going to happen.

With the mule, Daddy wasn't just thinking of the crops, he was thinking about the mule. He cared for it and often the mule ate before we did. But, if an unattended mule stepped into a hole and broke its leg, it would likely have to be shot. This was because horses and mules have so many bones in their legs that it is nearly impossible for a break to heal properly.

Daddy felt even more protective of us. He wasn't so

concerned with outside influences damaging our bodies. After all, Falkland was a pretty tame community. But, he was worried that exposure to harmful ideas and behavior might poison our hearts and minds.

Children are fragile and complex. One severe blow to our inner moral fiber might cause a break in our spirit that might never mend properly. So, Daddy took no chances. The only place we were allowed to spend time outside of church or school was with family.

Everyone's favorite place to go was to the home of Momma's twin sister, Aunt Sadie, because that was where Momma felt most comfortable. Even though they were twins—they were opposites. Momma was so white she could not be mistaken for black and Aunt Sadie had enough black features that she could not be mistaken for white. Momma didn't talk much, and Aunt Sadie was rarely quiet.

In fact, it was Aunt Sadie that taught us most of our family history. She was proud of it—shined the spotlight on it—whereas Momma left it alone.

Momma and her sister had babies at about the same time. Aunt Sadie and Uncle Hardy Diggs Wooten had 11 children—10 lived—Carrie Gray (who died as a child),Hardy Jr., Charlie Kurt, Bennett, Willie Roy, Bobbie Lewis, Charlene, Dennis Dean (DD), David, Sadie Best, and Lawrence. Momma and Daddy had eight children and seven lived. These two mothers adored each other's children. Even when we were away from

her house, Aunt Sadie would sometimes call one of us children on the telephone to say, "I just called to tell you that I love you."

It was in this safe environment—sharing love and the same strict moral values—that we spent many an evening playing tag in their yard or hide and seek in the barns. Then we'd come inside to have pillow fights or a friendly arm wrestle. There was always something to eat, someone to play with, or somewhere to explore.

The only thing I really missed at Aunt Sadie's was the television. Years back, the church members at St. John's Missionary Baptist had a disagreement. The church split. Momma and Daddy stayed at St. John's, but Aunt Sadie and Uncle Hardy helped found a new church—Friendship Free Will Baptist Church (now known as Friendship Holiness Church).

In fact, the church was built in their backyard—literally. Now you would think that Free Will Baptists would have more freedom than traditional Baptists, but they didn't. They could not watch television, play cards, or participate in sports, and the girls could not wear lipstick or wear dresses above their knees.

However, when they came to our house, while the adults purposely sat with their backs to the television, our cousins couldn't keep their eyes off of it.

Daddy often accompanied us to Aunt Sadie's. He and Uncle Hardy had been friends since childhood. When they were young men, Daddy and Uncle Hardy rode their bicycles from Falkland to Farmville—about 8 miles—to double date the twins.

When they hopped off their bikes, two of Momma's brothers hopped on to ride to see their girlfriends. Then, at the end of the day, Momma's brothers would return the bikes and Daddy and Uncle Hardy would ride back to Falkland.

No one knows for sure how Momma and Daddy met. Aunt Blanche seems to think they spotted each other at the movie theater. Whatever the case, Daddy claimed Momma as his bride on February 12, 1943, while he was on leave from the Army. Later, Uncle Hardy wised up and set his wedding date for September 22, 1943, but Daddy was not granted a leave. So Daddy—out of loyalty to his family and his best friend— actually went AWOL (Absent Without Official Leave) for the wedding and then sneaked back into Fort Bragg Military Base (about 100 miles away) undetected.

Even though there were 16 children in Momma's birth family, we only saw a few of them on a regular basis. Mostly, it was Aunt Sadie, but we also visited Aunt Bess, and Uncle "Puddin" Glaster Jordan.

I remember one afternoon at Uncle Puddin and Aunt Nina's, we were playing tag in the yard.

My cousin, Spanky, was "it" and I taunted him saying, "Nana, nana, na, na. You can't get me."

I was only about four feet away from him, but I was wiry and fast.

Spanky made a move and I made a move. Then, like a bull, he came charging right at me.

I turned on my heels and ran with all of my might. Unfortunately, I didn't notice the tree and ran head first into it! It knocked me out cold. The next thing I knew, it was dark and we were on our way home. Such were the ways of young boys in our family.

On Daddy's side of the family, we sometimes went to see his sisters, Aunt Mary Emma or Aunt Ethel, or his brother Uncle Mark. But, mostly we spent time with Aunt Helen. Like Daddy—Roy "Joy" Gorham—she had a wonderful spirit about her.

We've often wondered where she and Daddy got this from because Daddy never said much about his folks. In fact, Daddy only shared one story with us about his dad, Jack Gorham, born in 1879.

Daddy said that when he was a child, his daddy would take the mules and wagon to town once a month to buy flour, corn meal, lard, or the few things they needed. Along the way, he would get ahold of some stump hole whiskey. This was illegal moonshine hidden in tree stumps during the Prohibition, which lasted from 1919 (the year Daddy was born) to 1933. Granddaddy Jack would drink too much, get drunk, and fall off the wagon. Later that day, the mules would arrive at the front door as predictably as homing pigeons to their roost. A day or two later, Granddaddy Jack would straggle in.

The only thing we knew about Grandma Charity Dupree Gorham was that she had some Indian blood in her and that she

was 36 when she gave birth to my Daddy. Grandma Charity and Granddaddy Jack were sharecroppers and they raised 13 children in Falkland, not too far from our house. From all indications, Daddy and Aunt Helen had a difficult childhood, and yet they abounded in joy.

As a child, I used to study Aunt Helen. She always lived in poverty and yet in spirit, she was one of the wealthiest people I knew.

One day I asked Aunt Helen, "How can you be so happy when your life is so hard?"

I'll never forget what she said to me. She said, "You know, Bro, I can either cry or I can laugh. Neither one is going to change my situation. So I choose to laugh!"

I said a silent prayer. "Lord, give me what she's got. I want to be like that."

In all of our visits to family throughout my childhood, I never remember any of my relatives—adults or children— harming me in any way. We were considerate, supportive, and even protective of each other.

In fact, there was a very pervasive "Don't mess with my family" attitude on Momma's side of the family. Two of her brothers were shot and killed defending the honor of a sibling. Years later, when my brother, Walt, was newly married, he ran into our cousin, Linda Jordan. Walt introduced her to his new bride, Velma. Instead of giving the new bride a welcome hug, Linda looked the young woman in the eyes and threatened, "If

you ever do anything to hurt my cousin, I'll kill you."

That was the way the Jordans lived. If anyone did anything to one of us—they would have to deal with all of us.

In Daddy's household, we leaned a little more towards love and less toward violence, but we still stood up for each other.

I remember when I was in fourth grade, I wanted to buy three chocolate fudgsicles (chocolate ice cream on a stick) at school. I knew Daddy wouldn't give me a nickel for even one.

He'd say, "Boy, you need to know the difference between a need and a want. It's not my job to give you what you want."

So I got to thinking about Mr. Ellis' pear tree in the middle of his cornfield. He always told us kids that we could have pears as long as we did two things. First, we had to ask permission. Then, we were only allowed to pick up the pears that had fallen to the ground. I figured that he was concerned that we might get hurt if we climbed his tree.

So one day, after gaining permission, I brought along three tobacco sticks. I nailed them together to make one long pole and then carefully knocked down the most beautiful pears that I could reach. Once they hit the ground, I told myself, "I'm not breaking the rule."

I shined up the three prettiest, took them to school, and offered each one for sale for a nickel. Two boys bought pears and I had 10 cents in my pocket. Then, an older boy said he wanted one.

I said, "Here's the last pear. Do you have the money?"

He said, "Yes. It's in the classroom. Give me the pear and I'll go get your money."

I gave him the pear and then waited, and waited, and waited. I spent my whole recess waiting for this older boy to bring me my nickel.

Then the bell rang and recess was over. I realized that he'd lied to me. He'd stolen from me. I trusted him and he cheated me.

Tears began to pour out of my eyes and I couldn't stop them. Suddenly, my older sister, Madie Sue, appeared. She's the family protector. She will fight anyone.

Madie Sue bent over and asked, "Bro, what happened? Why are you crying?"

I told her the whole story and I could see her hands knotting up in fists. She knew who the swindler was and she was going to extract my nickel from him one way or another. Unfortunately for me, and fortunately for the boy, a teacher was nearby and Madie Sue had to abort her plan.

That evening at the dinner table, I told Daddy what happened.

He listened carefully, and then asked, "Boy, are you supposed to be selling things at school?"

"No. But I wanted some fudgesicles," I said.

He said, "Well, you still have two nickels."

I broke out in tears and said, "But I wanted THREE

fudgsicles!"

Madie Sue couldn't contain herself and said, "Daddy, it wasn't right what that boy did. He's in eighth grade and he stole a pear from a fourth grader."

Daddy studied my face. He thought about the cruel blow that this bully had delivered to his young son. Then Daddy applied the salve of wisdom to my wound.

As he shook his head, he said slowly, "Boy, there's nothing new under the sun." (Daddy was quoting King Solomon in the Bible.)

Daddy explained, "Since the founding of the world, people have been using these same tricks to distract and deceive people. Probably someone did it to him and now he's doing it to you."

I was hoping that Daddy would feel sorry for me and give me a nickel. But, he didn't.

As Daddy finished his dinner and prepared to step away from the table, he looked me right in the eye and told me man-to-man, "Boy, you're lucky that this lesson only cost you a nickel."

He smiled approvingly, letting me know that I would recover and be a stronger man for it. And, he was right. When I grew up, and was finally released into the world, I avoided many costly pitfalls by applying Daddy's simple wisdom.

SHARECROPPER'S WISDOM

Chapter 15

YOU CAN'T BRING THAT IN MY HOUSE

Daddy wasn't a very affectionate man. I never saw him kiss Momma, or say, "I love you." Even though we had three sofas in the house—one in every room except the kitchen—I never saw Daddy cuddled up with Momma. He didn't even hold her hand.

He was the same way with his children. We never heard the magic words. His hands were for working or disciplining. And yet, we knew that Daddy loved us.

One Christmas morning, there was a loud knock on our door. When Daddy opened it, I heard men shouting merrily, "Roy. Bet you never thought you'd see us again."

It was Daddy's Army buddies from World War II. They'd served in the 463rd Aviation Squadron together and forged a lifelong bond. But they were right; Daddy didn't expect to see them. Daddy was a different man than when they'd last saw him in the Army.

As they pushed forward to come into the house, Daddy smelled the "Christmas Spirit" on their breath and saw the six pack and bottle of liquor in one man's hand.

Daddy put his hand up and said, "You can't bring that in my house with my children."

The men looked a bit surprised. No, I think they were disappointed. Roy "Joy" Gorham used to drink and party with the best of them. But he and Momma had long since stopped doing that. As loyal Baptists, they no longer smoked, drank alcohol, or cursed.

As the men recoiled, Daddy smoothed things over. He told them, "I don't drink anymore. I can't have alcohol around my wife and children. But, we can sit here on the porch."

As they stepped backwards and then made themselves comfortable, I heard Daddy and the men talking and laughing. But I didn't listen in. I was replaying in my mind Daddy's words, "You can't bring that in my house with my children."

It made a deep impression on me. I thought, "Daddy values his family. You have to keep that stuff outside because I'm protecting my family. Friends or no friends, that stuff is not coming in here."

One day in the future, I would be saying those same words to my army buddies. Daddy showed me the way. He showed me how to stand my ground and put limits on what I allowed into my house.

Recently, my sister, Sarah, shared how Daddy courageously stood up to Mr. K.R. Wooten—our landowner.

Daddy had trained his children to greet Mr. K.R. Wooten when he visited our property. He would drive up in his big brown Cadillac to survey the crops. When he stopped his car, Daddy and the older girls would come up to his car.

The girls would say, "Hello, Mr. Wooten."

Mr. Wooten would kindly reply, "Hello."

Then, the girls would get back to work while Mr. Wooten and Daddy talked about the tobacco.

On one occasion, after the girls were out of earshot, Mr. Wooten told Daddy, "I'd like you to go to the ABC store in Falkland to get me some liquor. (ABC stores were established in North Carolina in 1935, shortly after the end of Prohibition, requiring people to purchase bottled liquor at these State regulated outlets. People could buy beer and wine at grocery stores and other convenience stores. As of 2016, North Carolina still operates under this code.)

Daddy said, "No sir. I'm sorry but I cannot. I never go into liquor stores."

His boss eyed him carefully. Mr. K. R. Wooten knew that my daddy was a deacon in the Baptist church. He also knew

that my daddy was a sharecropper—one step above a slave—and it was in his best interest to obey the landowner. On the other hand, Mr. Wooten knew that Daddy was a hard worker, honest, and a peacemaker.

Daddy held his ground, come what may.

After carefully considering his options, Mr. K. R. Wooten slowly replied, "Fine."

Then he added a warning, saying, "But I better never see you going in or out of a liquor store."

Sarah said that Daddy told her that story over and over again, but it wasn't until she grew to be an adult that she came to realize just how much Daddy laid on the line when he refused to compromise his values.

Chapter 16

HE'S IN A BETTER PLACE

Daddy scooped out the ice cream. One scoop for Lillie Gray. One scoop for Sarah Elizabeth. I watched as the frozen bands of vanilla, chocolate, and strawberry swirled perfectly around the spoon. Daddy carved out a scoop for Madie Sue, Vickie Lynn, and then skipped past me to give a scoop to my little brother, Walt. Then, Daddy served Momma and himself.

This was one time I didn't mind being served out of order. On this day, Sunday, February 5, 1967, I turned 11 years old. After everyone else got a scoop, my prize was the box and the remaining ice cream inside of it.

I took my first bite—vanilla—and felt the cool, creamy,

sweetness flood my taste buds. Then, I stepped it up a notch and carved out a spoonful of strawberry, careful to not get any chocolate on the edges. It was just like the vanilla, but with the added extravagance of strawberries. And then, my favorite—chocolate—rich, dark, creamy chocolate.

As I was enjoying my birthday bliss, Daddy slid a few penny cookies to each of us. Ice cream was such a rare treat. Daddy only bought it when one of us had a birthday. The birthday boy or girl got a serving plus the box.

When everyone else was done, there I was with my box. I tipped it up and let the melted liquid run over my teeth and into my mouth. Then I carefully took the side apart. My mission was to capture every single drop. I licked one side and as a drop began to run down the other side, I quickly flipped the box and caught it on my tongue.

When I was done, the box would be so clean that even a sugar seeking ant would walk by in disbelief. The inside of the box would be squeaky clean.

The only thing that would have made my birthday better was my sister, Joyce. This was my first birthday she missed because when she graduated, she moved in with Uncle Sim's son, LC, in Washington, D.C. so she could work. Little did I know that I would soon be seeing her again.

Uncle Sim and Aunt Blanche moved into our house when Joyce was just two years old. I was still a "hope" in my father's heart and wouldn't appear on the scene for a full seven years.

Daddy invited them to move into our four-room house after Uncle Sim had his third stroke and was left paralyzed. He lived with us for 17 years.

By the time I came along, Uncle Sim was pretty settled in. As I grew older, I didn't think much of the fact that he was confined to a wheelchair or the bed. He couldn't talk much, though if you irritated him, he would let you know.

He drooled a bit, had to urinate in a jug, and needed help with nearly all of his activities. Because he was a part of our family since my birth—I never thought anything about it. He was Uncle Sim. That was it. I never felt sorry for him— probably because I didn't know him before he lost his ability to walk or talk. I don't remember anyone feeling sorry for him. He just was who he was.

Vickie Lynn, who was three years older than me, probably had the most compassion for him. She actually slept in the room with Aunt Blanche and Uncle Sim on their sofa. When she was eight years old, Aunt Blanche "hired" Vickie Lynn to watch after Uncle Sim while she was at work and on weekends.

Vickie recently told me, "No one else wanted the job, so I did it."

During the summer, Aunt Blanche left Vickie money to buy Uncle Sim breakfast. Sometimes Aunt Blanche made him oatmeal. But he loved eggs. So mostly, Aunt Blanche left money for Vickie to walk to the Oscar Lee Bar and Grill to buy him an egg sandwich and some juice. For lunch, she'd head back to

the store to pick up a ham and cheese sandwich and a Sun Drop soda. Incidentally, Sun Drop is a North Carolina citrus soda, and it was Uncle Sim's favorite.

Then Vickie Lynn would brush his teeth, get him water as needed, and look in on him as she cared for her other duties around the house. In return for her work, Aunt Blanche bought all of Vickie's school clothes and nice Sunday dresses.

Sometimes Uncle Sim had seizures. About once a year, he would have to go to the hospital for a couple of weeks. Aside from that, he never left the house.

In November of the year that I turned 11, we were preparing our last lot of tobacco for market. The tobacco had gotten dry so the night before, we'd taken it out of the pack house to let the dew soften the leaves. The next morning we'd gotten up at 5 o'clock to repack the tobacco in the pack house so that it could be sorted and graded. About 9 a.m., Vickie decided to go back to the house to check on Uncle Sim.

Suddenly, Vickie came running back out to the barn.

She yelled, "Daddy, come check on Uncle Sim. I think he's dead."

Daddy ran to the house and sure enough, Uncle Sim had passed away.

Vickie later told me, "He was so sick and he'd nearly died so many times that I was kind of expecting it. But, it was still shocking."

Daddy saw the sadness and fear in his 14-year-old

daughter's face and gave his little girl a rare hug. Daddy assured her, "You will be all right. He's in a better place now."

I glanced in the room—just enough to see what all the commotion was about and then I high tailed it out of there. I was never afraid of Uncle Sim while he was living. But now that he was dead, my mind ran wild with thoughts of haints and ghosts.

Thankfully, Daddy did not have his coffin and wake at our home according to tradition. We just didn't have the room for it. Instead, Hemby Funeral Home took care of everything.

My big sister, Joyce, came home for the funeral with our cousin, LC Gorham. It was good to see her because she was one of my biggest cheerleaders.

It would be years before I would realize all the life lessons surrounding Uncle Sim. For one, family takes care of family no matter what. Uncle Sim had 12 siblings, but it was his baby brother—10 years younger—who would take him in. Loyalty—Aunt Blanche stayed true to Uncle Sim and supported their family, doing domestic work until the day he died. Waste not—live your life fully and courageously every day, for one day, if you live long enough you will lose your health, your energy, and your youth. Lick the box clean. Don't leave anything for the ants.

SHARECROPPER'S WISDOM

Chapter 17

GO GET 'EM

L et's go back to the double track, where the work is hard and the boss is mean, where the food is dirty 'cause the cook ain't clean," Daddy sang out joyfully.

This was our call to return to work. Lunchtime and playtime were over. Tobacco plants needed to be topped and suckled. It was mid-June and the flowering tops and immature new growth (suckers) were stealing all the nutrients. We had to pop off the flowering tops and then use our fingers to break the suckers with a motion similar to tickling the top of the stalk.

Even though we had to hand-prune 15 acres of tobacco— about 75,000 plants—it didn't feel like work. To me, it felt more like a race or a challenge to be like Daddy.

In a four-row section, Daddy took the two inside rows. Pop, pop, pop, pop. Facing toward the end of the rows, he'd reach to the right, pop and suckle, then reach to the left, pop and suckle. He looked like a machine. Pop, pop, pop, pop. Step and reach right. Step and reach left. So smooth. So fast. Not a drop of energy wasted.

Sometimes Daddy whistled or sang an old church hymn. This was Roy "Joy" Gorham at his best. He was my daddy and I wanted to be just like him.

When Daddy set us up for the afternoon work, he put my sister, Vickie, on the outside row facing me. She'd just completed her first year at Farmville High School, being the only black student in her grade. She was also a fierce competitor—being a celebrated basketball player during the season and then ostracized as an unwanted black in the off season. All of this made Vickie tough as nails.

Daddy purposely faced me opposite of Vickie. She was fast, but this 12-year-old boy could keep up.

We topped and suckled one plant at a time. Unlike Daddy, we had to face our plant, top and suckle, and then quickly side-step to the next plant. We competed with each other, but mostly our focus was on Daddy. We wanted to keep up with the man who'd learned to walk face forward doing TWO rows at a time!

My older sister, Madie Sue, who'd just turned sweet sixteen, and my younger brother, Walt, who would turn 11 about the time we were preparing the tobacco for market, were also

working with us. Daddy started them on a section just beyond the heap row—the wide row of dirt that the tractor drove down—placing Madie Sue and Walt on the outside rows just like he'd placed Vickie and me. Unlike Vickie and me, however, tobacco work did not bring out the competitive spirit in these two.

Like my brother Walt said, "I knew that when we got one row done, there was another one coming, so why rush!"

I inched my feet closer to the base of the plants, under the shade of the bottom leaves. This protected my "free feet"—my wonderfully bare feet—from the sunbaked dirt in the afternoon.

I glanced up at Vickie. She was just one plant ahead of me. She always wore shoes. And then I had to laugh when I thought of my daddy, about six feet in front of us. He wore shoes, but he always cut the leather, letting his pinky toes hang out to relieve the pressure from his callouses.

Pop and suckle. Pop and suckle. We all had on our worst clothes. Tobacco plants are gummy and they ruin whatever you're wearing. So, I was wearing my worst pair of newly retired school pants. We only got four pairs at the beginning of the school year, and no matter what, they had to last us until the beginning of the next school year.

By June, my pants were high waters—ankles showing—because I'd hit a little growth spurt. Not much, I was still a little runt, but an inch or two can make a difference. I hitched my britches up with a rope belt and then let my shirttail hang out because there was no one to make me tuck it in.

In looking back, I looked a bit like a living, breathing scarecrow, with patches on my elbows and knees. I didn't mind. That is what every other 12-year-old black boy in our community looked like.

My sisters, on the other hand, had long finished growing and they didn't put out their knees and elbows like us boys. This allowed them to look more presentable in the field. However, the gooey tobacco gum stuck to their clothes just like ours. At the end of the harvest, their field clothes could literally stand up in the corner just like ours!

Daddy wore old black dress slacks and a grey shirt. On top of his 5' 8" frame, he perched a hat—an old Fedora no longer suited for church. As I studied him, I realized that even in his field clothes and especially in his church clothes, Daddy looked dignified and handsome.

The way he dressed and the way he moved, Daddy was the definition of manliness—blending strength, grace, and productivity.

"How did he do it?" I wondered. He had huge hands—wore a size 13 ring—and a body that tipped the scales at 250 pounds, yet he glided effortlessly through the fields.

Pop. Pop. Pop. Pop. I could not figure it out. What is his secret? And then, before I knew it, we'd walked the length of a football field and finished the row. Daddy waited a few minutes for Vickie and me to finish our last few plants and then he'd say, "Go get 'em" and point toward Madie Sue and Walt.

We'd help them finish their rows and then we'd start the whole process all over again. It never occurred to us that Madie Sue and Walt weren't doing their share of the work. We were raised to work as a team and when Daddy said, "Go get 'em," we went and got 'em. We happily helped them finish their rows.

It would take me until I was a senior in high school to be able to keep up with Daddy, face forward doing two rows of tobacco at once. At that time, he was 55 years old and had less than a decade of life left in him.

That was my daddy. He was the man. In fact, I used to say, "I wish I could be just half the man my daddy is."

My sister Sarah's husband, Ronald D. Smith, corrected me when he heard me say that.

Ronald said, "JR, don't say that. If you grew up to be half the man your daddy was—he would be disappointed. Every man wants to see his children do better than him. Instead, you want to be TWICE the man he was."

That revolutionized my thinking. I thought about two guys I'd met in the library. One was George Washington Carver and the other was Booker T. Washington. Now, I'm not much of a reader, but it was required reading during Black History Month in elementary school.

What amazed me about George Washington Carver (1864-1943) was that he went from being a slave to being a scientist with a doctorate degree—all by hard work and perseverance. By the end of his lifetime, this black man had

helped millions of people of all colors worldwide and even met with three Presidents of the United States.

He had a broad vision—working out the benefits of crop rotation and nutrition—while staying hyper-focused on the peanut, developing over 200 products from this one plant.

George Washington Carver went way beyond his beginnings and that's what I wanted to do. His advice in the book said, "Education is the key to unlock the golden door of freedom."

George Washington Carver was actually invited to be the director of the Agriculture Department at Tuskegee Institute by my soon to be other hero—Booker T. Washington (1856-1915). This black man was President of Tuskegee Institute—but his work reached far beyond it. He was an author, orator, and educator who could build bridges between the white and black communities. He understood people and politics and could make things happen. It is said that he laid the groundwork for the Civil Rights Movement of the 1960s.

His most memorable quote for me was, "Character, not circumstance, makes the man." That's what these two men had—character. That's what Daddy had. And that is what Daddy was building in me. I believed that when I combined character with education, I too could make something of myself.

Chapter 18

NO SON OF MINE

Tobacco flowers are really quite beautiful—with long bases that flare open like the end of a trumpet—revealing a pink interior. Each plant is crowned with its own personal bouquet of a dozen or more blossoms, so an acre of tobacco can easily resemble a giant flower garden.

In fact, Better Homes and Gardens website features eight varieties of "cousins" to the commercially grown tobacco that make excellent additions to the family flower garden.

Depending on the variety, these flowering plants can grow to be anywhere from six inches to eight feet in height, and sport blossoms in a variety of colors including red, white, blue, green, and even an award-winning purple. And, they smell good

too. One variety—Jasmine Tobacco—smells like its namesake, one of the leading fragrances in the world of perfumes and cosmetics.

But, my Daddy wasn't growing flowers. His goal was to produce the biggest and heaviest leaves—especially at the top of the plant—to net the highest profit at market. To make that happen, he had to snap off the flower—called topping—so that the plant would redirect its energy into the leaves. In a nutshell, if Daddy had to choose between pretty and productive, he always chose productive.

So when I was 12 years old— with my ego in full bloom—Daddy topped me. It started out innocently enough. Walt and I were playing basketball in our yard with a few guys in the neighborhood.

"Over here, over here," my buddy, Stevie McDaniels, yelled as he jumped up.

He was open, so I threw the ball to him. Walt tried to block his shot, but it still went in.

"Swoosh!" I yelled. Oh, I was feeling good. I was on my way to being 13 years old, and as they say, I could smell myself. I didn't smell like a little kid any more. I had a man smell and now my man team was beating the pants off Walt's team.

Walt got the ball, dribbled about three feet, and then passed it to James Eason. James quickly threw the ball to Johnny Ray Dupree, but I was on him like white on rice. As Johnny Ray dribbled toward the goal, he kept one hand extended, warding

me off. I rushed forward in an attempt to steal the ball when he suddenly changed directions and we collided.

"Foul!" Johnny Ray yelled.

"What?" I countered. "That was no foul. You'd think you were fouled if a little fly landed on you."

"That was a foul, fair and square," his teammate, Johnny Earl Williams, argued.

Walt agreed, saying, "Bro, we all saw it. Let him take his free throws."

We were leading by 6 points, so I let the baby have his way. It felt good to stop for a moment and have a rest anyway. As I stood there panting, I could feel tiny rivers of sweat running down my face and advancing over my 12 visible ribs, before being absorbed into my black cotton shorts.

I heard the shot hit the rim and looked up just in time to see it bounce toward the house.

"Miss!" I yelled victoriously. "You know you're going to miss again," I added.

Then my team began rhythmically yelling, "Miss, miss, miss, miss."

Amid this racket, the shot went up and in without ever touching the rim.

"Swoosh," Walt and his team yelled in unison.

Walt looked at me and said, "How do you like those apples, Bro?"

"Lucky shot," I countered. "Our ball, and we still have

the lead by five. We'll show you boys how men play."

I had a good position, so my teammate, Bennett Gorham, threw the ball to me. I took a shot and the ball went around and around the rim before deciding to jump out. James Eason got to the ball before I did and quickly made a pass to Walt.

Walt was sweating worse than I was and as he dribbled quickly towards the goal, he suddenly stopped and stood there in a daze like someone had just unplugged him.

My teammate, Michael Eason, quickly grabbed the ball and Walt "woke up" just in time to hear Michael say, "Thanks, Walt. I just scored two points while you were sleeping."

The whole group burst out laughing.

Walt, realizing that he'd had another 30-second epileptic-like seizure, was furious. He didn't care who you were, how big you were, or what you thought you were, when Walt got mad, he was always ready to fight. So he came out swinging.

As he started flailing his arms around yelling, "You dirty rotten cheaters," it became even more hilarious. We were now dodging the "mad man" and the more he missed us, the madder he got.

Daddy overheard everyone taunting his youngest son. He sternly yelled from across the yard, "I'm not going to have that mess at my house, so leave! Every one of you leave. Now!"

That changed the mood faster than the DJ at our local radio station. My daddy was like their daddy. No one argued. No one ever talked back. Everyone did what they were told.

But I still wanted to play and I could feel the anger boiling up in me. As the guys began making their way from our makeshift dirt court to their shirts, I walked straight up to Walt and sneered, "You are always causing problems. This is all your fault!"

Then, like the first pink blooms on the top of a tobacco plant, seven bold words that I'd never uttered before, tumbled right out of my mouth and into Walt's ear.

"You little redheaded son of a bitch," I snarled. I got up in his face, glaring, silently daring him to hit me.

Walt turned away. He had a better idea. He walked right over to Daddy and reported, "Bro just called me a little redheaded son of a bitch."

I heard Daddy say, "What!," and then his heavy footsteps came pounding towards me. Now my friends, who were struggling to put their shirts over their sweaty bodies suddenly heard, POW! POW! POW!

Daddy slapped me across the face. He slapped me with his right hand and then his left hand, repeatedly sending my head from side to side like a punching bag.

At the same time, he was saying, "No son of mine is going to talk to anybody like that."

After he slapped me about 10 times, I thought he was done. But then Daddy grabbed my head and put it between his legs and started literally beating my butt. All the while, my friends, my man team, were watching me be beat by my daddy

like I was a two-year-old baby.

When he was done, I was so mad and in so much pain, that I just took off walking. I was walking and crying. I walked through the mule pasture, and into the woods.

With each step I was thinking, "I'm not going to live with a man who puts his hands on my face and beats me mercilessly and thinks he's my daddy."

I continued walking deep into the woods. I was running away. I could tell that the universe was on my side. The deeper my mood, the darker the sky until finally it was pitch dark.

I stopped walking. I accessed my situation. I had no food, no water, and no clothes except my soggy black cotton shorts.

To make matters worse, an owl hooted stirring up all the scary night sounds in the forest. It was at that moment that the severed bloom of my pride fell completely to the ground. And just like it happens with the tobacco plant, I felt my energy redirect itself to my inner core values.

As I marched steadily toward our house, I asked myself, "Where did that come from? I don't even believe in teasing people about their looks."

Walt was light-skinned and had auburn hair like our mother. I knew the teasing that children with unusual features endure, let alone a black boy with reddish hair.

"Why would I do that?" I asked myself.

I also knew that it wasn't Walt's fault that he had a

seizure. He had an illness. The doctor's even gave him medicine for it. It seemed like when he exerted himself, all the oxygen would leave his lungs, his eyes would roll back in his head, and he'd freeze for about 30 seconds. Then, it was like nothing ever happened.

My mind drifted to the time we were riding bikes together. It was just Walt and me. We were racing toward home, coming from Falkland, when suddenly he had an episode. He stopped peddling, stopped steering, rode right in the ditch and fell over.

He wasn't hurt and because no one was around, he wasn't embarrassed. He was just a little shocked. We laughed it off.

Little did I know that in the next year, Walt would outgrow this disorder just as the doctors promised. In the meantime, maybe I could have changed the whole outcome of the evening by standing up for my brother when he had his episode, instead of joining in the bullying. Maybe I could have been a better brother.

I don't know where S.O.B. came from. Even though I was in pain with every step from my beat down, I still had to audibly smirk when I thought about those words coming out of my mouth. In my Baptist house, saying S.O.B. was about the same as using God's name in vain. It was a major sin.

Maybe I was getting a little too big for my britches. By the time I reached the house, I'd humbled myself and decided that maybe it was not such a bad thing to live with Daddy. As I stepped in the door, the family kindly let me slip into bed without

any questions or comments.

It wouldn't be that easy when I met up with my friends over the coming weeks. They seemed to take pleasure in resurrecting the memory of my beat down and tossing it around like it was some kind of unfeeling football. But that taught me a valuable lesson too. I can live with embarrassment. It won't kill me and it too shall pass.

Chapter 19

DON'T BE LIKE A LOT OF FOLKS

D addy used to love to drive around Falkland, looking at miles and miles of tobacco fields. He wanted to see if his tobacco was coming along as well as everyone else's. I went with him a few times, but he drove too slow for me.

However, for my sister Vickie Lynn, driving with Daddy was her favorite childhood memory. It's odd how everyone is different. Of course, she will tell you that getting an ice cream at the end of the slow motion tour was definitely an incentive. But, mostly she enjoyed having Daddy all to herself.

"Daddy took the time to make me feel special," Vickie Lynn recently told me. "Daddy told me that God had given him

the gift of healing and that I also had the same gift. We were able to lay our hands on the sick and they would recover. I saw that happen with Daddy and I've seen that in my own life."

Daddy never used his time with me to make me feel special and he certainly never told me that I had a gift. Maybe it was because of my "are we done yet" attitude. Or, maybe he noticed that as we drove, I wasn't looking at the tobacco. I was looking at the houses and wondering to myself, "Why can't we have a house like that? Why can't we have a nice brick house with an indoor bathroom? I'd even settle for an ugly house with an indoor bathroom."

While I was silently coveting one day, Daddy said, "Boy, there's three tests a man has to pass, humility (keeping oneself low and teachable by self-topping), money, and women."

He tossed that line out to me like he was casting a sweet kernel of corn right under the nose of a 10-pound catfish. But I didn't take the bait. I didn't ask him to explain. I just let it drop like a seed in the soil of my mind.

Sometime later, it dawned on me that Daddy had not passed the three tests. He hadn't mastered money. That is why we lived in a little four-room shack with no bathroom. So, at the next appropriate time, I brought it to his attention.

That time came on a Sunday morning. I'd gotten my suit on early and was trying to entertain myself and stay clean by sitting on an old 5-gallon lard can that we used as a stool. I gently rocked it back and forth, hearing the thump, thump on

the kitchen floor as I moved to the right and then to the left. If I held on just right, I could actually "walk" the can across the floor without tipping over.

Daddy came in, noticed what I was doing but didn't comment. Instead, he said, "How do I look?"

"You look nice," I said, still focused on my can. I wasn't overly enthusiastic with Daddy because I was moving into manhood and didn't like being treated like a boy. My last beat down did a lot to distance me, but I was respectful. In my heart, though, I thought that my daddy was one of the most handsome and respected men in town. But I wasn't about to tell him that.

We had a few minutes and no one else was in the kitchen, so I tested the waters.

Still looking down at my feet, I said, "Daddy…"

He said, "Yeah, boy?"

"I figured out why we don't have any money."

Daddy waited to see what his brilliant 12-year-old had discovered.

As calmly as I could, I said, "Daddy, if we would start saving our money, we could have a nice house like the other people in our community."

I paused and Daddy didn't say anything, so I continued, "We give too much money away. Every Sunday, you make us put soft money (dollar bills) into the collection plate. That's a dollar for you, a dollar for Momma, a dollar for Madie Sue, a dollar for Vickie Lynn, a dollar for me, and a dollar for Walt.

Daddy that's six dollars a week. If we saved even half of that for a year we would have over $150."

Daddy still listened, but I could tell that I'd hit a tender spot. However, in all my youthful wisdom, I continued, "And then if you quit driving everyone around and giving people money—because you know a lot of those people make more money than we do..."

That was as far as I got. Daddy stepped forward and put his hands on my shoulders, quickly shifting my weight to the back of the can. Instinctively, to avoid tipping backwards, I moved my feet to the front of the can and strained to lean forward.

Daddy had my attention and he said sternly, "Boy, don't you be like a lot of folks that get all they can, can all they get, and then sit on the can." With that, Daddy took his hands off my shoulders and let the weight of my body seat the can square on the floor.

When I looked up, Daddy was gone. He was rounding up the family. It was time to head out the front door, walk east on West Avenue (Highway 222) for a quarter of a mile, and into the front door of St. John's Missionary Baptist Church.

On the walk—I pictured what Daddy was saying about the can. It was true. A lot of people store up money, and in our neighborhood it very well could be in a can—even a lard can. That would be a whole bunch of money, but if they just sat on it, it wouldn't help anyone.

Daddy was more like a river. Money passed to him and through him in a never-ending cycle. He did help many people, especially people who did not have any food. He even helped someone get his son out of jail. Thankfully, Daddy never had to do that for any of his own children. But this was a point that I would continue to disagree on with Daddy. There comes a time when a man needs to say no to others who don't plan, so that he can plan and save for his own children and his own future.

But Daddy got the last word in on this matter. Daddy said, "The Lord will give us what we need when we need it."

Two years later, we moved into a five-room house, with running water in the kitchen, though no indoor bathroom. It felt so spacious because my three older sisters had moved out and Aunt Blanche moved to D.C. when Uncle Sim died. So Walt and I had our own bedroom, Vickie Lynn and Madie Sue shared a room, and of course Daddy and Momma had a room. But now, we had a real living room.

And yes, Daddy eventually built a three-bedroom ranch, with two bathrooms, a kitchen/den combo, living room, laundry room, deck, and carport. He didn't do it by keeping money that he felt belonged to the church or by withholding a helping hand from neighbors in need. Daddy acquired his money by taking on another 20 acres of land when Mr. Harrell died. And then he took on an extra 40 acres when Mr. Bud Peaden died.

So by the time I was 14—living in the second house, Daddy was farming 100 acres with two sons, two tractors (a

John Deere and a Farmall), and a two-thirds sharecroppers agreement with Mr. Wooten. That meant that when the crops were sold, Mr. Wooten now only took one-third of the profits off the top, leaving Daddy two-thirds for his expenses and savings.

In 1976, when Daddy was 57 years old, he and Momma and Walt moved into his brick rancher—which was every bit as solid as the reputation he'd built in his community.

When I think back on the way Daddy's life came together, it was just like the song Momma used to sing when she was making a fire in the stove in the kitchen. She'd sing softly the 1950s gospel by Dorothy Love Coates, You Can't Hurry God, but she'd sing it her way.

You can't hurry God
Oh no, you just have to wait
You have to trust and give Him time
No matter how long it takes.

He's a God that you can't hurry
He'll be there so don't you worry.
He may not come when you want Him
But He's right on time.

Second Gorham family home.

sharecropper's wisdom

Chapter 20

YOU'RE BECOMING YOUR COMPANY

It's no accident when a man produces high-grade tobacco year after year. It's evidence of experience and understanding—often passed down from generation to generation—and solid work ethic.

Daddy had it all. He could "read the leaves" and they would tell him what they needed. If the tips of the leaves were turning brown, the plant needed more potassium. If brown spots began to dot the leaves, the plant needed more phosphorus. And if the leaves were shriveling up, it was a sure sign that there was a calcium deficiency.

The most important nutrient of all though, was nitrogen.

More than anything else, it affected the yield and the quality of the crop. If Daddy didn't add enough, the yields were smaller and the cured leaf was less desirable. Anyone grading the leaves could pinpoint the missing nutrient by noting the predictably pale color and slick poor texture.

However, if an inexperienced sharecropper got carried away with the idea that "if a little is good, then a lot is even better," he would be setting himself up for a lot of extra work. Too much nitrogen causes excessive suckering—robbers that need to be removed from the plant—and delays in maturity.

Daddy had the same knack with childrearing. I'm quite sure that this was not handed down from his parents. Instead, he seems to have gotten it from God himself, who promised in his word, "When my father and my mother forsake me, then the LORD will take me up. Teach me thy way, O LORD, and lead me in a plain path, because of mine enemies." (Psalms 27:10,11 KJV (King James Version))

Daddy expertly monitored the amount of church, school, and nearby relatives that he added into our lives. But, outside of that, I believe the single most important nutrient—our nitrogen— was a huge dose of hard work.

We took to the fields when we were nine years old— old enough to learn and young enough to have a strong will to please. Daddy started me out with the women at the bench, handing tobacco, and by the age of 10 I was so tired of their "girl talk" that I couldn't wait to get out into the field with the men.

During the priming season, I worked with Daddy 10 hours a day on Monday, Tuesday, and Wednesday. Then on Thursday, Friday, and half a day on Saturday, I worked for one of our neighbors, such as Mr. Bud Peaden. Now when I was working for Daddy, I was being trained and I was helping our family, so I didn't get paid one red cent. But, when I went to work for Mr. Peaden, he paid me $1.25 an hour. That meant that in two and a half long days, I made about $30.

So at the young age of 10, I started buying my own school clothes. I gave my entire earnings to Momma—just like every other child in our community—and she gave me back 10%. The 90% that she kept went directly for my clothes and my 10% went directly to my belly! I loved spending my money on store bought food.

Sometimes after payday, I would go to the store and lay out one dollar and seven cents. That bought me seven pounds of seedless grapes. I loved seedless grapes. If I bought them on Saturday, they would be gone by Sunday and I could account for every single grape. I didn't share any!

As I got a little older, Momma would give Walt and me a little longer leash. One time we were hanging out at a little store with our friends, Johnny Ray Dupree, Johnny Earl Williams, Dick Jones, and Bobby Ray Jones (sons of Big Man Jones). They were in the habit of loitering and I was just experimenting with the idea when Daddy pulled up.

"I think you boys need to get to the house," Daddy said.

"Why?" we'd ask innocently.

"Because you are becoming your company and you don't want to be like that," Daddy said.

What Daddy meant is that he didn't want us to hang around guys who were in the habit of hanging around. Daddy didn't want us to be "inoculated" with the common teenage plague—lack of ambition. As it was, we had an excellent reputation in our community.

People said, "Hire Roy's boys. Roy's boys get it done!"

We also got it done well, because just like he "read" his tobacco plants, Daddy watched his children for signs of "disease." At one point, I was so interested in being the first one done in priming (picking) the tobacco, that I started leaving part of the leaf behind.

As Daddy came behind me to inspect my work, he said, "Boy, you're leaving my money on the stalk."

Now this caught my attention, because I wanted Daddy to have more money. So when he called me over, I took a good look. Sure enough, part of the leaf stem was still attached to the stalk.

Daddy said, "I get paid by the pound and the first two inches of that leaf is where the weight is."

Daddy then took his hand and showed me how to reach in as close to the stalk as possible to pull off the whole stem. It was little things like that—attention to detail—that made me a valuable worker, even when I was very young.

At age 12, however, even though I enjoyed being paid by others and helping Daddy on our plot—I wasn't so sure that I wanted to grow up to be a worker. One time, I sneaked off to peek inside the local pool hall. It was about three-quarters of a mile from our house. I looked inside and saw men smoking, drinking, cussing, and having fun.

I thought, "That's what I want to do!"

I watched them for a good little while—wishing I could become their company—and I didn't really see any harm in what they were doing. No one was fighting. No one was doing anything bad. It was just a group of guys who knew how to have a little fun playing pool, having a cold one, and puffing away on that stuff that we were growing up the road.

I thought about stepping inside. I think the guys would have been cool with that. But then I thought about my daddy. He had a way of finding out everything. I knew that if I stepped in, he'd find out and I'd already been warned to stay away from the pool hall. I'd for sure get a beating. With that thought, I found myself turning around and literally running for home!

I also thought about joining the circus—or at least the fair. Nearly every October, just after we harvested peanuts, we went to the Pitt County Fair. Daddy gave us a dollar and whereas the girls later told me that they spent their money on popcorn, caramel apples, or cotton candy, I always spent my dollar on four rides!

Sometimes I'd ride the Ferris wheel, up to the top of the

world and then look down at the antlike people moving around on the ground. But I didn't choose this ride too often because, frankly, it was too slow.

I went more for the Tilt-A-Whirl which sent us careening toward opposing "cars" as gravity slammed our bodies from one side to the other, threatening to toss us out. Or the Zipper, which was so much cooler than the Ferris wheel, because we were locked in a cage and could spin around in circles while we headed for the sky, or when we looked like we were going to crash face first into the ground. And, of course, if there was a roller coaster—that was high on my list.

I saw all the easy money that floated around the fair. I thought, "These guys that run the rides must have a really fun life. Playing games, eating popcorn, traveling from town to town. That's the life."

But as you can imagine, my dollar was gone quicker than a scalded rabbit—leaving me to wander about the grounds looking at the latest tractors, the cleanest pigs, and the prize winning chickens.

Daddy would always make us leave by 9 o'clock, so we'd have to careen our necks to see the fireworks lighting up the sky through the back window of our car.

The next day, we'd be off to church from 9:30 in the morning, often till 2:30 in the afternoon. I tried that on for size too. Did I want to be a preacher? I was certainly in their company enough.

At church, I heard the same scriptures that I heard at home. "Honor thy father and mother." (Ephesians 6:2 KJV) "To obey is better than sacrifice." (1 Samuel 15:22 KJV) "Give, and it shall be given unto you; good measure, pressed down, shaken together, and running over." (Luke 6:38 KJV)

But I decided that a preacher's life was not the life for me. However, I could go so far as to get baptized. So when I was 12, we drove to Farmville and I was baptized in a little pool. This was a step up from when my sisters were baptized. They had to wade into Tysons Creek, next to Short Bridge Primitive Baptist Church.

Speaking of water—that reminds me of another tedious chore that Walt and I had to do. And me, being the older one, I had to do the brunt of the work. On wash day, we had to draw water from the well. Literally, we lowered a one-gallon bucket about 20 feet into an open well. When the bucket was full, we pulled on a chain that ran across an overhead pulley and hoisted up the full bucket to the top of the well. Then, we took it to our washing machine on the side porch—only a few steps away. Thankfully, the washing machine had electricity, because hauling water was difficult enough.

Each wash day, we did four loads of wash. So we had to haul about 20 buckets for each load of wash, for a total of 80 buckets. Then, we had to haul an equal number of buckets for the rinse cycle. Not only was it heavy work—one gallon of water weighs eight pounds—it pretty much burned up the day

doing one load after another.

All in all, Daddy kept me busy with a large dose of hard work, but not so much that I developed "suckers"—undesirable work avoidance behaviors that would have to be removed from my personality.

In time, I figured out what Daddy meant when he said, "You are becoming your company," and I learned to use this for my advancement once I joined the army.

Daddy and Momma in latter years.

Chapter 21

NO ONE CAN MAKE YOU HAPPY

L ife started turning in my favor at the age of 14. By then, in 1970, Farmville High School was fully integrated. My sisters, Sarah Elizabeth and Vickie Lynn, had plowed the fields of social change, removing the big rocks and breaking up the sunbaked soil of resistance with their iron-like perseverance.

By the time I arrived on the high school scene—with 110 black students and 78 white students in the freshman class—the soil was moist, loose, and ready for a new crop. But what could I do to be a leader like my sisters? How could I be like Booker T. Washington and George Washington Carver—leading the way of change?

I decided to run for vice-president of the school. That's right. Aim high and see what happens. I only knew a handful of students and I was no expert on school politics, but I submitted my name for the ballot.

Imagine my surprise when I won! That was a huge boost to my self-esteem. In fact, I'm pretty sure that I was the first black student ever elected as vice-president of Farmville High School. Immediately, I was catapulted from a "freshman nobody" to giving daily announcements for the school. President Jean Wells—a white senior in Vickie Lynn's class—was easy to work with and she let me lead a Student Government Association (SGA) meeting in her absence.

I no longer operated under the mode of "see what happens." I took my responsibility seriously and helped the student government team make things happen. In the process, I regularly met with the top leadership at the school—accelerating my training as a leader.

With that under my belt, I looked for further involvement at school by trying out for the basketball team. The coach kept me until the final cut—probably out of regard for my superstar sister, Vickie Lynn—but I just didn't have the skillset for the game.

At first, I took the rejection pretty hard. I wanted to be involved in sports. I wanted to be part of a team. Suddenly, I thought of something Daddy told me earlier.

Daddy said, "Boy, if you are willing to do what other

people won't do, then you can go where other people can't go."

In the crazy workings of an adolescent boy's mind, I crossed that with another saying of Daddy's, "There's three tests a man has to pass, humility (keeping oneself low and teachable by self-topping), money, and women."

Suddenly a plan formed in my mind. I went to Coach Scott and asked, "Can I be the water boy for the varsity basketball team?"

He studied me carefully. New freshman with the "big head syndrome," because 8th graders are the alpha dogs of middle school, newly elected vice president of the entire school, big sister who held the glory spot on the girl's basketball team, and here I was asking him for the lowest and often time laughed at job of being a water boy?

Before he could say no, I mustered all my humility and said, "I promise I will be a good water boy. If I can't play on the team, at least let me support the team by being the water boy."

I think it amused him, but he said, "Okay. You can be the water boy."

In time, my humility was tested. Some of the kids laughed at me and sneered, "You're the water boy? Ha. Ha. Ha."

When that happened, I'd look them right in the eyes, and ask, "How many away games do you get to go to? I get to go to all the home games and all the away games for free."

Then, I'd raise my eyebrows, smile slightly and quietly add, "I think that's pretty smart if you ask me."

My calm and logical response—spoken with full confidence—gave my "opposers" a new perspective—and THAT is what leadership is all about. Frankly, the first time those words spilled out of my mouth, it took me by surprise, but since it worked so well, I kept using it.

That year, when Thanksgiving came around, I was feeling pretty good about myself. I was the firstborn son, I was vice president, and I was moving up in the world.

As I sat on the back porch—pondering my good fortune—the smell of baked turkey and stuffing wafted out an open kitchen window. Suddenly, the only thing on my mind was food.

I walked into the kitchen as casually as possible and surveyed the room. Walt was sitting at the table, while Joyce C. tended to the turkey. On the counter were six sweet potato pies, freshly baked from Momma's own hands.

"What you want, Bro?" Joyce C. asked suspiciously.

"Nothin. I just came inside to get a drink," I said. In this house, we had water that ran to our sink by an electric pump from the well. We still didn't have an indoor bathroom, but this house was a lot better than our first house.

As I sipped my water, Walt and Joyce C. eyed me wearily. So, I finished that glassful and filled my glass again.

Finally, Joyce C. turned away from the hot stuffed bird and I silently swooped in to snatch a bit of stuffing.

The next thing I knew, Joyce C. demanded, "Put it back,

Bro!"

I held my ground. "I'm not putting nothin back."

"Put it back," Joyce C. insisted.

I looked her right in the eyes and repeated slowly, "I'm… not… putting… NOTHIN back!"

Suddenly, I heard a much deeper voice say, "Bro, you heard what she said. Put it back."

I looked over my shoulder and here's my kid brother, Walt, ordering me around.

I cocked my head and said, "Who do you think you are?"

Walt walked toward me and I'm still thinking I'm the big brother. I'm not sensitive to the fact that in the last year, he's grown bigger than me. He gives me one more chance.

He repeats clearly, "Put it back."

I get out the first two words, "Make me," when suddenly Walt grabs me by the shirt and lifts me up. I can't get away. I am held powerless by my….little…no… younger brother! I was so mad that three days later Daddy wanted to know what in the world was wrong with me.

Walt and Joyce C. told him the whole story. Then Daddy had a little talk with me.

Daddy asked, "Why are you so mad at your brother? Why do you let him control you like that?"

I looked at Daddy in disbelief and said, "He's supposed to be my little brother, but he's so big he can beat my butt."

Daddy countered, "I don't mean physical control. I

mean mental control. Why do you let him do that? You've been mad for three days. Why are you letting him control you?"

"I don't know what you mean," I said.

"If Walt causes you to change your behavior, that means that you are allowing Walt to control you. You can't allow people to do that to you, Boy," Daddy said.

I was thinking about that, not really grasping it, when Daddy continued, "Boy, no one makes you happy, no one makes you mad, no one makes you depressed. All of those are your choices."

"But Daddy, Walt made me mad when he grabbed me," I said.

Daddy patiently explained, "No. You chose to be mad and then you chose to stay mad. The truth is, you woke up in a good mood on Thanksgiving Day. If Walt did something or said something that caused you to change your behavior or your attitude, then you allowed him to control you. You made a choice. It's always your choice."

It would take me years to fully assimilate this wisdom from a lowly sharecropper, called Daddy. But it did give a clue as to how Roy "Joy" Gorham managed to stay happy, regardless of external circumstances. It was actually pretty simple—he made the choice. But that is also the hard part—to hold to a logical choice and put out the wild flame of emotion while your "enemy" is trying to ignite it.

Not that Walt was my enemy. Actually, he was a good

little brother and for the most part, he wanted to get along. In fact, when we were grown, he virtually apologized for growing bigger than me saying, "When I was having my seizures, the doctor told Momma and Daddy that the medicine would cause me to sleep a lot and eat a lot. I actually grew 5 inches in one year when I was in elementary school."

I don't know if it was the medicine or not. I really think it was just in his DNA, because by the time Walt started high school, he was 5'10" and 155 pounds. He was built like a machine, with a six pack that he never worked for, and natural athletic ability that helped him excel at basketball, football, and track.

Contrast that with me—I started high school at 5'3" and 105 pounds. In fact, the biggest thing on me was my afro. Yet, in time, I found my sport.

Actually, just a couple weeks after Thanksgiving, my health and physical education teacher, Coach Ronald Vincent, brought out the wrestling mats and put all of the boys in a circle like a bull in a ring. Then, he called out two names. Whoever got the takedown (bringing the opponent to the ground) stayed in the ring. When he finally called my name, I got the takedown. So, he put me up against every boy in the class—many of them much bigger than me—and I took everyone down.

I owed my skill to the never-ending church and BTU (Baptist Training Union) meetings. While the grownups were doing their stuff inside—I was outside with my buddies, tussling.

That's what we called it, tussling. For us, tussling is wrestling in a suit in such as way as to do the most damage (overpowering) to your opponent, without damaging anyone's clothes.

So when the coach saw me use my Falkland church skills to overpower my Farmville opponents, he said, "James, tomorrow when you are done cleaning up the balls for the basketball team, I want you to come down here to roll around on the mat with my guys on the wrestling team."

I said, "Sure."

So the next day, I go down and see that everyone on the wrestling team is white except David Ebron. He's my same weight—105—so Coach Ronald Vincent has me wrestle with him. I beat him in points, got the takedown, and David couldn't get up.

I didn't really think anything about it, but the next day, when I was cleaning up the basketballs, Coach Vincent came up to me and said, "James, catch."

I looked up, caught a little ball of nylon cloth and asked, "What's this?"

He said, "It's a wrestling uniform."

I said, "I'm not on the wrestling team."

He said, "You are now!" Then he added, "The guy you wrestled yesterday, didn't come to school today. Before I take a forfeit tonight, I'm going to let you wrestle."

I said, "But I'm not on the team."

He says firmly, "James, you're on the team. Incidentally,

we are wrestling at Camp Lejeune."

Before I know it, he's gone and I'm left to put on this little uniform. All the while, I'm thinking that we are going to Jacksonville to wrestle Marines. My stomach is in knots, but I'm determined to see this through.

When I get on the scales, I am one pound over. I weigh 106. My Coach talks to the other coach and says, "Hey look, can you give me a pound? My guy just joined the team yesterday. This is his first meet, so it will give us a chance to see what he can do. Can you give us a pound?"

The other coach agreed and so I wrestled at 106. So here I am—the ultimate rookie—and I beat the "marine" in points. So now, I have the big head. I'm really something! So the next week, I'm officially on the team and we go to Smithfield-Selma High School. My opponent is originally from upstate New York and he's been wrestling for six years. I go out there and he wipes the mat with me. He didn't pin me but he beat me 9 to 0. He beat me bad.

After the meet, Coach Ronald Vincent came up to me, put his hands on my shoulders and said, "James, you've now experienced the glory of victory and the agony of defeat. Now, you are ready to become a good wrestler. Now I'm ready to train you. You're ready for your training."

And he did train me. He pushed me beyond what I thought I could do and I put everything on the mat for him, because he took time to build a relationship with me for the two

years that he coached me.

On the way to a meet, I'd ride on the bus right behind him. When it was my turn to wrestle, he'd say, "Go get them, Hippie (my high school nickname)" and I went and got them. I'd do everything I could to win.

Then, on the way home, the bus would stop at a fast food restaurant, like Hardee's. (Wilber Hardee opened the first Hardee's Restaurant in 1960 about 10 miles from Falkland, in Greenville.) All the guys would jump off the bus and then the coach would turn around and say, "Hippie, you hungry?"

I'd say, "Yah coach."

He'd say, "Got any money?"

I'd say, "No coach."

He'd take me into Hardee's and buy me a Hardee's Husky Burger—a big, juicy, charbroiled burger on a sesame bun—fries, and a drink. He had no idea what that did for me.

I'd say to myself, "This guy really cares about me. He buys me store bought food. My own parents can't do that for me."

Then, when we'd get back to Farmville High School, many times my daddy would not be there to pick me up. So, Coach Ronald Vincent would go eight miles out of his way to make sure that I arrived home safely. I can't tell you how many times he did this in the two years that I wrestled for him.

But what I can tell you is that he was fully invested in me. He wanted me to be a good wrestler. So he rode me, pushed

me, and demanded that I give 100%. And I gave him 100%. I didn't hold anything back. I had so much respect for him that if he said I could do it, I believed that I could do it. In doing this—he became my second daddy. He didn't take the place of my daddy—but he had the second most powerful influence in my development as a young man and future leader.

Incidentally, I became so wrapped up in wrestling, that I let my English grade slip…or should I say crash. It was shortly after I joined the team that I brought home a report card with an "E" on it.

When Momma saw that, she said, "Bro, you bring this up to an "A" or you come off the wrestling team."

There was no way that I wanted to come off the team and though this was the only time I ever remember Momma getting involved in my school work, she was not negotiating. So I talked to my teacher, Mrs. Cox. I buckled down and did all of my work—but to get my grade up to an "A," my teacher gave me an option to memorize and recite to the class The Creation—a 598 word poem by black poet James Weldon Johnson (1871-1938).

Not only was Johnson a writer, he was also the first black elected to lead the NAACP in 1920 and the first black professor to be hired by New York University in 1934. Clearly, he was my kind of role model, so I took the assignment willing.

Even though this opportunity was offered to the entire class, I was the only one that accepted it. In the process—I got my "A" and continued wrestling.

Two years later, when I wrestled for Coach Linwood Woodard, I took all of Coach Ronald Vincent's lessons and all the commitment to the next level. By the time I graduated, the wrestling team was reversed—all black guys with only one white guy. I collected a shelf full of trophies and placed 4th in the state of North Carolina.

My only regret is that Daddy never came to a meet. He never got to see me wrestle or see the referee raise my hand in victory. It wasn't that he didn't want to. But at that time, our conservative Baptist faith prohibited involvement in sports. As a deacon, Daddy felt that he had to support the church, but as his son, he let me make my own choice. Also, Daddy and Momma did attend our annual awards banquet and see us get our awards.

When I left high school, I never had a chance to thank Coach Ronald Vincent for all that he'd done for me. Years later, I was invited to be the keynote speaker for the 2010 graduating class at my alma mater, East Carolina University.

Before the speech, the University hosted a breakfast in my honor for family and friends. Daddy couldn't be there because he'd passed away 27 years earlier. However, as I walked into the room—in my full Brigadier General uniform—there sat Coach Ronald Vincent.

He stood up and said to me, "Hippie, I always knew that you would make something of yourself."

Tears streamed out of my eyes. I had not seen this man for 38 years and for him to be here and to say what he said

was a very emotional moment for me. He played such a key role in shaping my life in my freshman and sophomore years, and now he was here to let me know that he was still watching me, still believing in me, still wondering what I would do next.

General JR Gorham & Coach Ronald Vincent,
Former Wrestling Coach Farmville High School
reminisce as JR prepares to deliver 2010 Fall
Commencement address at East Carolina University.

SHARECROPPER'S WISDOM

Chapter 22

IF YOU DON'T DROP IT

In 1917, World War I drove demands for cigarettes to new highs, causing tobacco prices in Pitt County to rocket from 13 cents to 35 cents a pound. In other words, farmers' paychecks almost tripled. Two years later, when Daddy was born, Falkland tobacco soared to 53 cents a pound. However, the following year, it plummeted to 21 cents. It's pretty easy to see how all of this could wreak havoc on a sharecroppers' finances.

According to Pitt County records, in 1930, local tobacco held at 30 cents a pound even though the Great Depression—which began on October 24, 1929 with the stock market crash—was deeply entrenched. But, in 1931, tobacco prices plummeted

to an all-time low of 8 ¼ cents a pound. I shudder to think about how Daddy—age 12—and his 12 siblings survived through that year. But they did.

That got me realizing that a man could sow the same seeds in the same soil, and harvest exactly the same crop—and yet his profits or losses were dependent on factors outside of his control. So, what did sharecroppers do? The tradition in my family line is that they never gave up. They kept sowing and harvesting, year after year, hoping and praying for better times.

Better times arrived in the form of a new leader, President Franklin D. Roosevelt. He signed into law the US Agricultural Adjustment Act of 1933 (AAA) to stabilize tobacco (and other commodities) by regulating acreage restrictions (limiting the amount that could be grown) and paying subsidies (a cash payment to the farmers to prop up the market value of tobacco). That program was recently phased out in 2014, but it helped tobacco growers during Daddy's lifetime.

However, even with the AAA, Daddy had to contend with fungus, bacteria, viruses, insects, and unfavorable weather. The fact is, in years of poor harvests we didn't buy clothes, we ate more rabbits, fish, and squirrels, and we certainly didn't go to the Pitt County Fair.

Of course, I didn't really understand all of this when I was a knuckleheaded 16-year-old boy. I was just interested in getting my life started. I had places I wanted to go, people I wanted to meet, and I definitely wanted to get out of this podunk

town called Falkland.

My first goal was to learn to drive and I had this under my belt. When I was about 10, Daddy bought an old John Deere Tractor and by the time I was 12, he had a Farmall too. So Daddy let Walt and I drive the tractors—unassisted—to plow fields.

When I was 14, I decided to drive Daddy's truck. Of course, Daddy never would have allowed that—being a law abiding Baptist deacon—so I "borrowed" his truck while he was at church.

I sat in the front seat, found the drive and the reverse, and then took off down the dirt path. Driving was a cinch—nothing to it! I imagined that Daddy's truck was mine. Well, not exactly. In reality, I was a bit embarrassed of Daddy's raggedy old truck. But, I imagined that I was driving a car, a nice slick, fast car and I was waving to all of my friends—in my imagination. Before I knew it, I was at the end of my path. So I coolly slipped the truck into reverse so I could turn around and head back. Unfortunately, I backed too far, sliding into the ditch.

The more I tried to work my way out, the deeper the truck sank. Suddenly, my mind zipped back to when I was seven and had stolen a sip of Daddy's coffee—but I wasn't seven and this wasn't coffee.

My mind raced faster than the tires—when they weren't getting any traction. And then I came up with a plan. I'd ask Walt to bring the tractor down to pull me out. Surprisingly, we

were able to hook chains up to the tractor, pull Daddy's truck out, and put everything back where it belonged before Daddy came home. Even more amazing is the fact that Walt had something on me, but he didn't snitch to Daddy.

Two years later, I finally came of age for driver's training. I passed the classroom instruction shortly after my 16th birthday and completed the required drive time in the summer. With that done, my final hurdle was to go to the Department of Motor Vehicles (DMV) in nearby Farmville to get my driver's license.

Now, Daddy was not one to let me get out of farm work to run an errand, but he was agreeable to take me during our 2-hour lunch break, provided we would be back by 2 o'clock. So before we walked to the fields, I pulled out the wash tub that Walt and I used to bath in—about 11 inches high and 26" across the middle—and filled it with 12 gallons of cold water from the hose. Then, I worked the tobacco until noon.

As soon as Daddy gave the call, I ran to the house, threw bed sheets up on two clothes lines to create instant walls for my outdoor bathtub, and then jumped in the now sun-warmed water. Incidentally, I was the oldest, so Walt had to use my dirty bath water when I was finished. The girls, on the other hand, bathed inside using a foot tub that only held about 5 gallons of water.

After I was squeaky clean and dressed, Daddy drove me to Farmville. I passed the printed test easily. The only thing that stood between me and my driver's license was the driving test. I climbed in the car, adjusted my mirrors, buckled my seat belt,

and eased onto the road. I drove with my right hand and I drove with my left hand—letting this evaluator see what an expert driver I was. When it came to the three-point-turn, I executed it flawlessly—using only one finger!

When we returned to the DMV, the examiner said, "Mr. Gorham."

"Yes sir," I said eagerly.

He said, "I have to inform you that you flunked the test."

I said, "Do what?"

He said, "You failed to drive safely. You failed to keep both hands on the steering wheel."

When we got back home, my neighbors and my brother were already in the field priming tobacco again. So when my dad and I walked up, my neighbor, Douglas Dupree, hollered, "Did you pass?"

I said, "No. I flunked."

Walt started laughing at me. He said, "Bro, I thought you could drive. Ha. I thought you could drive."

I went at him—ready to land all the disappointment that I was feeling right on the side of his head—when Daddy grabbed me.

Daddy said, "Boy, you better drop it. If you don't drop it, it's gonna drop you."

Daddy was warning me to control my anger, or my anger would control me, and no good ever comes from vengeance. So I shook it off.

To make matters worse, about two weeks later, Daddy took me back to Farmville to take my driving test again. The same examiner slid into the passenger's seat, but this time, I had everything covered. I kept both hands on the wheel and executed everything perfectly.

At the end of the drive, he said, "Mr. Gorham."

I replied confidently, "Yes sir."

He said, "You failed again. You took way too long on that three-point turn."

I was crushed and I thought to myself, "I didn't know there was a time limit on the turn."

As you can imagine, announcing this was even more painful the second time. As soon as my baby brother heard, he cracked up laughing and said, "I thought you could drive. Not only did you flunk once, Bro, you flunked TWICE! Oh, God, I can do better than that and I haven't even had driver's education."

Oh, I was steaming mad. I wanted to run him over like a mile long freight train—altering his mind and body so much that he wouldn't even recognize himself in a mirror. But once again, Daddy was there.

Daddy told me again, "Boy, you better drop it before it drops you."

But Walt didn't drop it. Walt kept egging me on. He used non-verbal communication—rolling his eyes and smirking—which translated to mean, "How can you be so stupid!" Because

he never said the words, his actions flew under the radar of Daddy's surveillance.

So, I boiled silently—taking Daddy's advice—and endured the humiliation.

Daddy, perhaps suspecting that the examiner was targeting me personally—knowing that I was a black grandson of the white Mr. Jim Bundy of Farmville—had another idea.

"Why don't you take your test in Greenville," Daddy said gently. "That will give you a fresh start."

"No," I said adamantly. "I'm going to get my driver's license under this examiner, even if I have to take my test 10 times."

So, Daddy took me back to Farmville and the third time was a charm. I had the same examiner, took the same road test, but this time I passed.

Pretty soon after that, Daddy bought me a two-tone white and green 1963 Ford Galaxie 500. Actually, this was the third set of wheels that Daddy gave me. First, when I was nine years old, I begged and begged for a bike. All of my buddies had bikes and I knew how to ride, but I didn't have my own wheels.

That Christmas, when the girls went into Momma and Daddy's room to get their presents, Daddy told me to go look in the kitchen. There, against the wall was an old, ugly, hand-painted green girl's bike. But it was MY bike and I quickly changed my clothes and rode down the path.

When I found my buddies—who all had new three-speed

English racers—they helped me put cardboard on the front forks to beat against my spokes just like theirs.

No one ever teased me—probably because I was so powerfully proud that I could now go where they went. And though I could see the vast difference between our rides, I knew that my daddy gave me the best he could. In fact, it was the Salvation Army that made Daddy a hero that year and to this day, I cannot pass a Red Kettle at Christmas time, without dropping in money.

Two years later, Daddy went to the W.W.Wooten Store and bought me a brand new 36" candy apple red and bright white bicycle for $35. Of course, Daddy didn't pay Mr. Wooten $35. He bartered and traded his labor and then paid $15 cash. But that is how a man of small means makes dreams come true for his family.

Now, before me, stood a Ford Galaxie 500. It wasn't exactly mine, but since I was the only one who could drive, it was like my car. It was older—a 1963—in 1972, but it had a fast front end. The car actually looked like it was moving when it was standing still. Instead of having the front hood and front bumper squared off on the front, the hood actually hung out a bit—like the head of a shark.

Of course, one of Daddy's motives was to have me drive a car load of choir members while he drove another to various churches for special events. I didn't mind driving them, but I couldn't get over the fact that Daddy was now spending twice

as much money in gas hauling everyone for free, while we still lived in a house with no indoor bathroom.

However, Daddy let me drive the car other places too, but I had to buy my own gas. Momma helped out by letting me keep most of my money from field work and during the school year, I drove a school bus. After putting gas in the car, I put some of Cuttin' George's delicacies in my stomach.

Home of Cousin George where he served countless plates of chitterlings and barbeque for $2.50.

For $2.50, Cuttin' George would load up a plate with stewed chittlins (hog intestines), barbequed pork, slaw, and a slab of cornbread. On the weekends, people lined up in his yard to get a plate full of this goodness. Years later, long after I'd moved from Falkland, I would stop by Cuttin' George's for a plate of memories that never grew old.

By the time I was 16, beatings from Daddy were a thing of the past—though my resentment continued to smolder. But he had other, more subtle ways of keeping me in the right lane of life.

One Friday night, I went out with my buddies. When I came in at midnight, Daddy opened the door for me. I know that he smelled the alcohol on me, but he didn't say a word. Instead, at 6 a.m. he called me out of bed to go to work just like it was any other Saturday morning.

He put me on the John Deere tractor and told me to "break ground." By 10:30—bouncing up and down in the seat plowing the frosted ground—I was sick. I started throwing up. By noon, I was feeling considerably better, so I downed two hot dogs, a batch of fries, and a soda at Oscar Lee's Bar and Grill. That was a big mistake. We went back to work at 2 o'clock, and by 3:30, I was throwing up again.

Daddy kept me on that tractor until 7 o'clock—all the while knowing how sick I was. When I got home, I cancelled all my Saturday night plans and went straight to bed. The next day, I

was back in church—fully aware that my drinking went against the church and against Daddy. I made a resolve that I would never do that again. Not so much because I was concerned about the church or Daddy—but because I never wanted to be that sick again and I never wanted to miss another Saturday night of fun.

However, three months later when we were priming tobacco under the blazing hot sun, I did it again. And just like the first time, Daddy knew it, and he made me work through it.

About this time, I was feeling quite manly—quite capable. On the mat, I could over power opponents—winning the favor of my classmates—and confirming my extraordinary skill. In the tobacco field, I could prime tobacco almost as quickly as Daddy—one of the fastest primers I'd ever worked with.

So when a neighbor asked me to help prime his field, I agreed. But when he drove Walt and I home for lunch, I asked, "How much are you paying us?"

He said, "Same as last year, $1.75."

Determined to improve my situation and knowing that I was one of the fastest primers in the area I said, "Excuse me, Sir, but I need $2.00. What I'm doing is worth $2.00 an hour."

He said, "Well, I'm paying $1.75."

Walt and I jumped off the truck, ate our lunch, and then waited until 1:30. The man drove up and blew his horn. Walt ran out—still willing to work for $1.75.

The man said, "Is your brother coming?"

Walt said, "Not unless you're paying $2.00."

The man drove off and I stayed home. I was proud of myself for taking a stand and holding my ground. But I was a little miffed that I would have 5-hours of pay missing from my wallet on Saturday night.

Daddy didn't find out what I'd done until he came home that evening. I told him what happened and I assured him that I would find another job in the morning. Daddy was fine with my plan to find more work, but not with my attitude to promote myself.

He said, "Son, let me tell you something. You are never going to amount to much of nothin if you keep doing what you just did. You're never going to win. You're a little black boy and you can't get ahead with that attitude. This is what you need to do. When you get a job, you bust your butt to get your boss promoted. The reason you do that is because when he gets promoted, that will create a vacancy. The person who worked the hardest to help him is probably the one he is going to refer to fill the vacancy. His recommendation will go a long way. Your job is to get your boss promoted."

At the time, Daddy may as well have been talking to the wall because the connection between my ears and my brain were still plugged with resentment. However, the curiosity of such an odd recipe for success stuck in my mind until years later, when it could sink into the soften soil of my heart. Only then, did I realize the full potential of these wise words, and put them into

practice in my careers at First Citizens Bank and in the North Carolina National Guard. True to Daddy's promise—this was one of the most valuable keys to my success.

sharecropper's wisdom

Chapter 23

THINK LONG AND HARD ABOUT THAT DECISION

Daddy understood the growing cycle. No matter how well intentioned a sharecropper is, if he plows and plants in the frozen and low light conditions of January—it is all for nothing. The ground simply will not yield and the seed will not grow.

Like many teenagers, I entered the January of my youth in my senior year of high school. The relationship between Daddy and me had been growing steadily cooler and I gradually discovered that I knew more than this man who was stuck in the past—or so I thought.

Unlike the early years of my life—when I was so eager

to soak up his wisdom, gain his approval, and be just like him—I now wanted nothing more than to leave his "prison," escape this so-called town of Falkland, and make my mark on the world.

Looking at my role models—Booker T. Washington, John Weldon Johnson, George Washington Carver, and Martin Luther King, Jr.—I knew that education was the key to upward mobility. So I applied to and was accepted to North Carolina A&T State University in Greensboro, North Carolina.

However, just prior to graduation, my friend, Rick Streeter, and I contracted a bad case of senioritis. We decided to play hooky from school. At the end of our romp, we planned to quickly slip into the Army recruiter's office to pick up a "we were here" signature—to make our whole plan permissible.

Our adventure went as planned, until we entered the recruiter's office. That Sergeant painted such a glowing picture of travel to foreign lands in faraway places doing heroic deeds, that we signed up that day. We didn't ask our parents anything. We just did it! That was May 10, 1974, and it was one of the best decisions I ever made in my life.

I still had my heart set on education, but here is the sweet part. If I signed up for two years, instead of making Daddy pay for my education, the G.I. Bill would cover it. This is because I enlisted during the Vietnam War Era.

Just as a side note, this was a tumultuous time in American history. In fact, the day before I enlisted, Congress began the impeachment process against President Richard M.

Nixon for his role in the Watergate scandal. Then, three days before I arrived for duty in August, he became the only U.S. President to resign from office. In the meantime, the Vietnam War—raging from 1955 and peaking in 1969—was further dividing the country.

Our family watched the 6 o'clock CBS news every night and listened to anchorman Walter Cronkite report the latest Vietnam body count. And two popular songs in the 1960s demonstrated the polar extremes of the American people regarding the war. The first, The Ballot of the Green Berets, sung by SSGT Barry Sadler still gives me goosebumps every time I hear it. Listen to it on YouTube and feel the pro-war pride. Then, listen to the number one hit on the Billboard Top 100, War, sung by Edwin Starr. This equally passionate song became one of the top anti-war songs ever. It was in this era—tightly entwined with the Civil Rights Era—that I decided to enlist.

Back to the recruiter's office, the Sergeant promised that if we signed up for three years, my best friend and I would serve in the same place for the first 18 months. Rick and I chose the three-year deal.

When I came home that night and announced my decision at the dinner table, Momma was shocked and disappointed.

She said, "You did what?" She added, "Bro, you are college material."

Daddy said nothing, but he was grinning like a Cheshire

cat. He was proud that his oldest son was following in his footsteps. Daddy had served during World War II in the United States Army 463rd Aviation Squadron, earning four medals and a rank of Corporal in his tour of duty from October 1, 1942 – February 16, 1946.

Within a few moments, I was able to assure Momma that I was still going to pursue my education—but on Uncle Sam's dime. That didn't seem to comfort her much. I suppose to her, war is war—always a risk of injury or death—and the longer we put off our goals, the greater the chance of losing sight of them.

With my escape plans written in ink, I found myself relaxing a bit with Daddy. I continued to be subject to him— working the tobacco and other crops—throughout my final summer. Just to demonstrate how hard core my daddy was, he had me priming the last of the tobacco crop up until the day before I had to report for duty.

On Saturday, August 10, 1974, after we'd primed the last of the tobacco, Daddy said, "Bro, it's 2 o'clock and I know you have to leave tomorrow for the Army. So go ahead and take the car to see your girl, but be home early so you can go to Sunday school tomorrow."

I didn't say a word, but I thought to myself, "What! I'm a grown man, 18 years old, going into the Army and I can't get a break in this place?"

I made it in by 11 o'clock, got up the next day and went to church with my family. After we ate dinner at 6 o'clock that

evening, I was in Greenville catching the Trailways bus to Fort Jackson, South Carolina.

I'm saving all the details of my Army career and all the wisdom that I learned for my second book, but suffice it to say that within a short period of time, I fell right on my big fat head. The first thing I did was everything Daddy tried so hard to keep me away from—smoking, drinking, carousing, playing pool, and letting loose.

Then anger started to bubble up—anger that I'd suppressed as a teenager—and it began to poison my entire life. I started using alcohol to soothe all my pains and treat all my symptoms to the point that I was on one big, continuous drunk.

On December 24, 1976, just six weeks before my 21st birthday, my life reached an all-time low. I actually considered suicide. Then, a miracle happened, spawning a new decision. I told myself, "This is as low as I ever go. From this day forward, I am only going one way and that is up."

I'm saving that miracle for my next book, but know that I took immediate action. The day the community college reopened from winter break, I enrolled in an English and a math class.

The Army changed me in so many powerful ways. I grew physically, finally enjoying that growth spurt that Daddy had promised. I went into the Army at 5' 8" and 137 pounds, and three years later came out at 5'11" and 175 pounds.

Mostly though, I grew emotionally. I realized the source

of my anger towards Daddy. I was so focused on material riches and our lack thereof, that it blinded me to the priceless assets that my family gave me. I was raised in a home with old-fashioned values, with two parents who were determined to protect me from the vices of youth, and in a church family and huge extended family that genuinely wanted the best for me. This was my rich soil—my heritage—and in this kind of soil, I could now chose to grow whatever crop of life that I desired.

When I arrived in Falkland at the end of my duty on August 12, 1977, things had changed at home too. Gone was the shotgun house with no indoor bathroom. Daddy built a brand new three-bedroom "rancher." Five years later, he parked his first brand new car under the carport. Daddy finally got what he and Momma always wanted, but he did it without robbing his children of their future. By getting his priorities straight, Daddy got it all.

Within a few days of coming home, I started attending East Carolina University (ECU). Life was good. Uncle Sam was paying for my education and Momma and Daddy agreed that I could live at home. On top of that, I found a job on campus at the Student Supply Store.

My next big turning point happened on the first day of my sophomore year in college. I purposely walked into my Spanish class a few minutes late so I could survey the clientele. Immediately, my radar zoned in on two beautiful black women. One was especially fine on the outside, but from first glances,

she seemed a bit empty on the inside. The other, Barbara Jean Battle, was attractive physically, but it was her inner spirit that my heart latched onto. Within 10 seconds, I was already hatching a plan to change her last name to Gorham.

The 3rd Gorham family home which was built in 1976 while I was away in the army.

House Three

It was then, with the newly softened soil of my heart, that Daddy began to sprinkle seeds of wisdom.

Daddy said, "Boy, when you find the gal that you think you want to spend the rest of your life with, think long and hard about that decision. From that one decision will come 90% of your happiness or 90% of your misery."

Daddy then repeated something he'd told me when I was a teenager. Daddy said, "When you find your gal, don't be so concerned with spending time with her at the movies or going out to eat or those kinds of things. There will be plenty of time for that later. What you want to do—if you are really serious—is spend as much time as you can in the house where she grew up. You want to observe the relationship between her mother and her father. This is what her expectation of married life will be. That is all she's ever seen. See how her mom treats her dad and see how her dad treats her mom."

Daddy was on a roll now. This was probably to date the longest conversation we'd ever had. He continued, "If you don't understand the dynamics, then you are going to have a long row to hoe. You've got to understand the relationship between her mother and her father. That is very, very important."

My mind drifted back to a few years prior when I was 20 years old, in the Army, and I had married quickly. It was singularly one of the biggest mistakes of my life. The disaster was all over in 18-months, but Daddy was right, this poor union with a young lady in basic training accounted for 90% of my

misery at the time. If I'd followed that one piece of Daddy's advice, I would have aborted the whole situation. But, I was still in my January season and both of us were at fault for the failure.

Daddy paused and then said, "Bro, there are two things you have to do if you want a good marriage."

That caught my attention. I said, "Two things? Enlighten me."

Daddy said, "Number one: Don't go places that you cannot take your family. If your family can't go, then you don't need to be there. Number two: Don't do things you can't do with your family. If your family can't do it, you don't do it. Now that is easy to say, but it's hard to do. But if you do it, you will avoid 90% of the problems married folks get themselves in to."

It took seven years for Barbara and I to sign the marriage license (September 13, 1986), and it would be too late for Daddy to attend our wedding. Daddy would never get to meet my first son, Tony Witherspoon Gorham, from a previous relationship, or the three children from the union of Barbara and me, our daughter Jamie Royelle Gorham, or James Roy Gorham II (who only lived eight days), or my youngest son, Joshua Caleb Gorham. But, he did get to meet Barbara before he died.

One Saturday, in 1980, about six months after Momma passed away on January 20, I drove Barbara to Falkland. She was the only girl that I ever took to meet Daddy. We stayed and talked for less than an hour.

When we got ready to leave, just as I was opening my car door, Daddy grabbed me by the sleeve and said, "Come here, boy."

I followed him a distance and he softly said, "Boy, if you're smart, you'll hold on to her."

I said, "Really?"

He said, "Yeah."

I said, "Daddy, we've been here less than 45 minutes. Why do you say that?"

Daddy smiled knowingly and affirmed, "I know what I'm talking about. If you're smart, you'll keep her."

I smiled at Daddy in disbelief and lightly said, "Whatever."

Then I hopped in the car and we drove back to campus at ECU. However, his words stuck with me. I thought to myself, "Daddy must have seen the same thing in her that I saw the first time I laid eyes on her."

Backing up to the fall of 1977, at the same time that I'd been discharged from the Army and started attending East Carolina University, I also joined the North Carolina Army National Guard. It was the oddest thing, but only 29 days after being "free," I missed the uniform. The National Guard was the perfect solution for me.

This opened up the opportunity to attend Officer Candidate School. In 1980, through hard work and determination—I graduated Distinguished Honor Graduate. At the ceremony,

Daddy was overflowing with pride. I do believe that this was one of the happiest days of his life, to see his son on stage with Generals being honored in a way that few officers—black or white—ever achieve. Little did he know that one day, his son—James Roy Gorham—would be a General, the first black Brigadier General of the North Carolina National Guard.

Shortly after this event, Daddy and I took a road trip to Washington, D.C. On the five-hour drive there and back, Daddy told me his life story—man to man.

Daddy said, "I used to get drunk and I used to party."

Daddy said this about himself, but he somehow knew that I was living the same way—footloose and fancy free. As a single man, I figured that I'd better get it out of my system. Daddy then told me that he continued this behavior, even after he was married. In fact, he told me of one incident that sticks in my mind.

Apparently, he was seeing a young woman while he was in the Army, and neglected to tell her that he was married. On his last visit, a letter from Momma slipped out of his coat pocket and landed silently on the floor.

As Daddy told it, "I was sitting there, laid back in the chair relaxing, when all of a sudden I felt a cold blade on my throat."

The woman screamed, "Why didn't you tell me you were married! I'm going to kill you!"

He started pleading with her to no avail and finally was

able to knock the blade away from his throat and escape.

He said, laughing now at the absurdity of the event, "I left my coat and everything and never went back."

Daddy's voice then took on a serious tone and he said, "Bro, it took me years into my marriage to get my life straightened out. Your Momma and I used to go to the juke joint and get so drunk that one time when we were driving, we hit a curve, and the jolt threw your oldest sister Joyce C. out of the car. That was a wake-up call. But it was years later, and only after I made a commitment to the Lord, that your Momma and I cut out the foolishness and straightened up."

What I took away from that was that Daddy understood how I was living at the moment as a single man. He was also telling me that I would get past this. This would not define me. I would get to the same level that Daddy reached when it was my season. That gave me a sense of hope.

Daddy also let my sister, Lillie Gray, see another side of him. When she was 20, she found herself pregnant out of wedlock.

As Lillie Gray told me, "I was living in Brooklyn, New York at the time and I wrote a letter telling my parents goodbye. I didn't feel that I could ever return to Falkland, because this would be such a disgrace and a shame for our family. I knew that Daddy was a deacon in the church and a well-respected man of God in the community."

Instead of shunning her, our parents encouraged Lillie

Gray to come home. Once there, Lillie Gray felt completely welcome. She slid right into her former role of being "Daddy's helper"—a bit of a tomboy who helped repair the equipment around the farm and the house.

One day, when they were fixing the brakes on the truck, Daddy said to Lillie Gray, "It's at a time like this that you need to be with family, no matter what people say or think. The most important thing to do is to come home and allow your family to support you."

He then told Lillie Gray that women can die in childbirth. It is no time to be going it alone. Daddy reminded her that his own sister, Mandy Gorham, died due to complications from childbirth and it devastated the whole family.

"Daddy then made me promise," Lillie Gray continued, "to never pull away from family in a crisis. Instead, lean on your family and depend on them, because most of the time they are the ones who will stand by you through thick and thin."

Daddy's compassion and honesty forever changed his relationship with his daughter.

Lillie Gray said, "Daddy was always my Rock, but on that day, he became my confidant."

In 1982, my brother, Walter Louis Gorham, married Velma Cloud. He too, had an opportunity to learn Daddy in a whole new way. After Momma passed, Walt, Daddy, and I lived in Daddy's house as three bachelors. We related to each other less as father, son, or brother and more man to man. We joked, had

fun, and even went on double and triple dates.

When it came time to choose a best man for his wedding, Walt had to look no further than his own father. Walt said, "In my mind, Daddy was the best man in my life. In fact, he was the best man I ever knew."

Shortly after graduating from college, I bought a house in Winston-Salem. However, I still made the three-hour, 175-mile drive to Falkland to see Daddy.

My last visit was on Monday, July 4, 1983. I came bearing good news.

I said, "Pops, I just got promoted. I'm now a First Lieutenant in the National Guard and I'm an officer at First Citizens Bank."

As I stood their glowing, waiting for Daddy's smile of approval, he asked, "Son, are you tithing (voluntarily giving 10% of your earnings to the church)?"

I said in disbelief, "Do what?"

Daddy repeated, "Are you tithing?"

I said, "No."

He shook his head and then caught my eye. He said, "Son, you are not the sharpest axe in the shed. Who do you think is responsible for all those blessings you just told me about? Can't you give back 10% of everything you make because God is blessing you?"

I said, "Yes sir" with my mouth, but that was only to get him off my case.

He shot another question at me, "Do you go to church on Sunday?"

My eyes widened as I thought to myself, "I'm 27 years old and in my estimation, I'm doing the best that I can."

Before I could get any words out, Daddy continued, "Boy, the Lord gave you 365 days a year to do anything that you want to do. Can't you give him 52 of those back? Can't you at least go to church on Sunday?"

I said, "Yes Sir," but I had no intention of following through on my word.

When our conversation was over, I headed back to Winston-Salem, a bit disappointed at Daddy's reaction, but nonetheless glad to see him.

Three days later, about 7 o'clock in the evening, a call came in from Barbara. She was still at East Carolina University, finishing her degree.

She said, "JR, I have some bad news. Your father had a massive heart attack and he's dead."

I went numb. My legs started to give way and I collapsed into a chair. I thought to myself, "I just saw Daddy three days ago. He was so full of life and suddenly he's snuffed out."

In that instant, my life changed. I thought, "He's always been here and now he's gone."

I sat in shock for a while. But, after I regained my bearings, I grabbed a few things and headed home. Somewhere on Interstate-40, between Greensboro and Burlington, I

remembered my promises to Daddy. I made the decision right then that I would attend church on Sundays from this day forward when at all possible, and I would tithe 10%. I've been doing that now for 33 years.

Daddy died on July 7, 1983 at the height of tobacco season. He had 12 acres ready to top and prime. So his seven children—mostly professionals ranging in ages from 36 to 25—went back to the fields to bring in Daddy's final harvest. We drove in from as far as Washington D.C. and Maryland every weekend for eight weeks.

If I ever had the spirit of my daddy, it was then. I worked like a slave and never tired. When we primed a row and got to the end, I'd say, "Let's go guys. We've got to get this done."

They sometimes pleaded, "No, let's take a break."

I encouraged them to continue, saying, "No, we've got to get this done."

Everyone helped, including some distant relatives who'd moved into our second house in Falkland. They had four children and while Ricky and Randy helped Walt and I prime, their sister, JoAnne, drove the tractor. Aunt Helen—still the Rock—helped in the field with some of our sisters, while others cooked the meals. Then, our cousin, Victor Gorham, helped us cure and market the tobacco.

It was just as Daddy would have wanted it. It was his final lesson to get us to work together, to come to the aid of one another for the good of the family.

As Daddy once told his firstborn, Joyce C., "I'm not always going to be with you, so you need to be there for one another."

Our family—much of the time under the care of Joyce C.—really is there for one another. We travel across the states to make sure we attend graduations, award ceremonies, surgeries, family reunions, and even an annual retreat for the women in the family.

I look back now at all the doors that Daddy opened for me. In 1993, I walked through yet another door that Daddy was barred from. I'd gotten word that Mr. W. W. Wooten had taken ill and was on his death bed.

I walked up to his house—showcased right in the center of town—and intentionally walked up the walk to the front door. I sensed people looking at me, questioning, "Who does he think he is?"

I knocked boldly on the front door. When the housekeeper opened it, she looked at me like I was the first black man to ever try to enter this house by the front door.

I smiled, letting my banker's suit introduce me, and said, "May I see Mr. Wooten please. I'd heard he's very ill and I know that if my Daddy was alive, he would want to come see him."

She took my request to Mr. Wooten and he received me. He knew who I was, not just by name, but by sight. I'm a splitting image of Daddy—just five shades lighter. We had a

pleasant conversation, in which I wished him a speedy recovery. He died on May 26, 1993 and with him, died the pre-Civil Rights Era.

I realized that a man sees things differently when he is closer to the exit of his life than to the entrance. In all fairness, Mr. W. W. Wooten was not a hard man. He was a decent man in all of my encounters with him. He never treated me rudely and he never looked down on me. He was just a product of his time, and that time had passed.

Even the town of Falkland changed. Though it still boasts a population of less than 100, on October 3, 2012 Falkland, North Carolina earned a place on the National Register of Historic Places. The online pdf of the application reads, "The present-day physical character of Falkland is conveyed by a combination of buildings from its pre-Civil War origin through its mid-twentieth-century growth, making it the best example of the country's remaining historic rural communities."

I have to thank Daddy, the town of Falkland, all the heroes I met in the books in the library, and so many people who came into my life, for helping me become the man that I am today. As my spiritual father, Bishop J.C. Hash, once told me, "You can teach your children what you know, but you are going to produce who you are." Daddy was a masterful leader in his day and he produced leaders of tomorrow.

Now I find myself in Daddy's shoes. He cultivated wisdom on the same 100 acres in the same little town for his

lifetime. I, on the other hand, gleaned my lessons as a marathon man who navigated my way to the top of military and corporate careers that took me around the world.

In my next book, I'll take you on my journey—letting you relive my adventures, feeling the full weight of my disappointments, and soaring to the elusive heights of victory. Through it all, you will discover for yourself the sweet seeds of success, which you can cultivate in your own life.

Seen here in this newpaper photo with Daddy, I was a Distinguished Honor Graduate of OC 22 and received the Leadership Award.

My family: Tony, Jamie, Me, my wife Barbara and Joshua

ABOUT THE AUTHOR

General JR Gorham's passion for leadership began as a small child. Like most young leaders, he believed that leadership was all about him. Thankfully, he had Daddy—sharecropper Roy Gorham—who set him straight.

Armed with the hard-earned character traits of humility, respect, service, faith, hope, endurance, and compassion—JR's peers and superiors consistently chose him to lead.

At the age of 14, this freshman won the election to serve as vice-president of the Farmville High School. From that year forward, he stayed involved in student government. Then, at the age of 18, he joined the United States Army and later the North Carolina National Guard.

Fast-forwarding, by the age of 55, JR Gorham was the first black officer to be commissioned as Brigadier General of the North Carolina National Guard. Simultaneously, he excelled in the banking industry and was ultimately promoted to Vice-President of First Citizens Bank in Kernersville. Currently, General JR Gorham serves as Director of Special Projects in the N.C. Department of Public Safety.

JR earned a bachelor's degree from East Carolina University, married his college sweetheart Barbara Jean Battle, and became Daddy to Tony, Jamie, and Joshua. He holds a master's degree in strategic studies from the U.S. Army War College.

His extraordinary wealth of personal experience and education, coupled with his warm, Southern charm, makes JR a favorite motivational and leadership speaker with young people and business leaders. To contact General JR Gorham visit his website and Facebook page SharecroppersWisdom.com.

ABOUT THE CO-AUTHOR

Patty Jo Sawvel, co-writer of *Sharecropper's Wisdom*, worked with General JR Gorham to preserve in ink and E-copy the message that he'd written on the tablet of his heart. In the process of capturing his father's legacy, we discovered that General Gorham has an entirely new crop of wisdom from his own life experiences! Award-winning writer, Patty Jo Sawvel, has been recognized twice by the North Carolina Press Association for her work as an investigative reporter. Her book *Under the Influence: The Town That Listened to its Kids* won the 2014 Global Ebook Award's Gold Medal in the non-fiction current events category. Her services include interviewing, co-writing, editing, layout and design, and publishing. For more information go to www.ClassicWritingPR.com.

"Roy Gorham masterfully planted tiny seeds of wisdom— usually less than 12 words per lesson—to shape the attitudes and outcomes of his children. Those same potent seeds sprang to life in my heart as I helped preserve his legacy for future generations. Perhaps his greatest lesson is the reminder that character—grown in the soil of our hearts—is the basis for everything of value that we produce." —Patty Jo Sawvel

References {In Order of First Use}

"The Year 1956 From The People History." What Happened in 1956 Inc. Pop Culture, Prices and Events. The People History, n.d. Web. 01 Dec. 2015.

ECONOMIC HISTORY OF PITT COUNTY 1690-2012 (n.d.): n. pag. Pitt County Development Commission. Web. 01 Dec. 2015.

"Potter's Raid on Greenville, Tarboro, and Rocky Mount, July 19-23, 1863." Potter's Raid on Greenville, Tarboro, and Rocky Mount, July 19-23, 1863. "THE NORTH CAROLINA HISTORICAL REVIEW," Volume LXXIII. Number 1. January 1996, n.d. Web. 05 Dec. 2015

"Brown v. Board of Education." History.com. A&E Television Networks, n.d. Web. 11 Dec. 2015.

"Civil Rights Movement." History.com. A&E Television Networks, n.d. Web. 11 Dec. 2015.

"John F. Kennedy - Civil Rights Movement." John F. Kennedy - Civil Rights Movement. N.p., n.d. Web. 11 Dec. 2015.

"Martin Luther King, Jr." Bio.com. A&E Networks Television, n.d. Web. 11 Dec. 2015.

"The Greensboro Sit-In." History.com. A&E Television Networks, n.d. Web. 11 Dec. 2015.

"Pitt County Chapter of the NAACP." Facebook N.p., n.d. Web. 11 Dec. 2015.

History, Office Of Archives And, and Department Of Cultural Resources. Falkland Historic District (n.d.): n. pag. Web. 11 Dec. 2015.

"Welcome to Pitt County Government Online." Welcome. N.p., n.d. Web. 11 Dec. 2015.

"The Pledge of Allegiance." WA Secretary of State. N.p., n.d. Web. 02 Jan. 2016.

"North Carolina Alcoholic Beverage Control Commission." Home - North Carolina Alcoholic Beverage Control Commission. N.p., n.d. Web. 02 Jan. 2016.

"George Washington Carver" Bio.com. A&E Networks Television, n.d. Web. 02 Jan. 2016.

"Booker T. Washington." History.com. A&E Television Networks, n.d. Web. 02 Jan. 2016.

"How to Grow Flowering Tobacco" Better Homes and Gardens, , n.d. Web. 02 Jan. 2016.

"Dorothy Love Coates." Wikipedia. Wikimedia Foundation, n.d. Web. 15 Jan. 2016.

"Parasitic Diseases." Tobacco. INRA Science and Impact. N.p., n.d. Web. 15 Jan. 2016.

"Fertility – Nutrients | North Carolina Cooperative

Extension Tobacco Growers Information." North Carolina Cooperative Extension Fertility Nutrients Comments. N.p., n.d. Web. 15 Jan. 2016.

"James Weldon Johnson." History.com. A&E Television Networks, n.d. Web. 15 Jan. 2016.

"Agricultural Adjustment Act." Wikipedia. Wikimedia Foundation, n.d. Web. 16 Jan. 2016.

"Vietnam War History." History.com. A&E Television Networks, n.d. Web. 20 Jan. 2016.

"Historical Events in 1974 (Part 3) - OnThisDay.com." OnThisDay.com. N.p., n.d. Web. 20 Jan. 2016.

"Ballad of the Green Berets - [HD] - - - SSGT Barry SADLER." YouTube. YouTube, n.d. Web. 20 Jan. 2016.

"War" by Edwin Starr (Original Video - 1969)." YouTube. YouTube, n.d. Web. 20 Jan. 2016.

sharecropper's wisdom

SHARECROPPER'S WISDOM

SHARECROPPER'S WISDOM